60 Juices and Smoothies Recipes for Home

By: Kelly Johnson

Table of Contents

Juice Recipes:

- Green Citrus Blast
- Tropical Paradise
- Berry Bliss
- Carrot Zinger
- Refreshing Cucumber Mint
- Beetroot Apple Energizer
- Citrus Carrot Glow
- Cranberry Orange Refresher
- Pomegranate Mint Quencher
- Watermelon Basil Splash
- Grapefruit Mint Cooler
- Kiwi Lime Splash
- Turmeric Pineapple Wellness
- Mango Passion Paradise
- Strawberry Basil Bliss
- Blueberry Lemonade Quencher
- Carrot Pineapple Ginger Zing
- Minty Melon Cooler
- Cucumber Kiwi Refresher
- Raspberry Peach Paradise
- Apple Ginger Pear Refresher
- Cantaloupe Basil Bliss
- Turmeric Orange Carrot Crush
- Pineapple Mint Cucumber Quencher
- Strawberry Kiwi Kale Kick
- Pear Berry Citrus Splash
- Cucumber Pineapple Mint Delight
- Blueberry Lavender Lemonade
- Gingered Watermelon Lime Quencher
- Mango Basil Beet Boost

Smoothie Recipes:

- Berry Blast
- Mango Tango
- Green Power

- Chocolate Peanut Butter Delight
- Pineapple Coconut Bliss
- Blueberry Almond Bliss
- Cherry Vanilla Dream
- Spinach Pineapple Protein
- Mint Chocolate Chip Delight
- Peachy Green
- Raspberry Almond Protein
- Vanilla Berry Delight
- Green Tea Mango Fusion
- Peanut Butter Banana Power
- Orange Carrot Turmeric Elixir
- Chocolate Banana Nut Smoothie
- Mango Coconut Chia Delight
- Pineapple Spinach Sunshine
- Banana Berry Protein Boost
- Cherry Almond Smoothie
- Mocha Banana Coffee
- Raspberry Mango Coconut Dream
- Green Avocado Pineapple Powerhouse
- Blueberry Walnut Bliss
- Peach Raspberry Chia Refuel
- Pineapple Banana Turmeric
- Coconut Blue Spirulina Elixir
- Orange Carrot Mango Glow
- Chocolate Cherry Protein
- Raspberry SPinach Almond Bliss

Juice Recipes:
Green Citrus Blast

Ingredients:

- 2 cups spinach
- 1 cucumber
- 2 green apples
- 1 lemon (peeled)
- 1-inch piece of ginger

Instructions:

Prepare Ingredients:
- Wash all the fruits and vegetables thoroughly.
- Peel the lemon and cut it into quarters.
- Peel the cucumber if desired and chop it into manageable pieces.
- Core the apples and cut them into chunks.

Juicing Process:
- Set up your juicer according to the manufacturer's instructions.
- Begin by juicing the spinach. You can alternate handfuls of spinach with the other ingredients to ensure an even mix.

Juice Cucumber:
- Follow with the cucumber chunks. Cucumbers add a refreshing taste and contribute to the overall hydration of the juice.

Juice Green Apples:
- Juice the green apples. Apples provide natural sweetness and complement the earthy flavor of the spinach.

Add Lemon for Citrus Flavor:
- Juice the peeled lemon quarters. Lemons add a zesty citrus flavor, enhancing the overall taste of the juice.

Include Ginger for a Kick:
- Finally, juice the 1-inch piece of ginger. Ginger adds a subtle spicy kick and offers potential health benefits.

Mix and Serve:
- Once all the ingredients are juiced, stir the juice to combine the flavors.
- Optionally, you can strain the juice if you prefer a smoother texture, but keeping the fiber from the spinach and apples is beneficial.

Serve Chilled:
- Pour the Green Citrus Blast juice into glasses over ice.

- Garnish with a slice of cucumber or a twist of lemon for a decorative touch.

Enjoy:
- Sip and enjoy this refreshing and nutrient-packed Green Citrus Blast juice!

Feel free to adjust the ingredient quantities based on your taste preferences. This vibrant green juice is not only delicious but also rich in vitamins and minerals. Enjoy!

Tropical Paradise

Ingredients:

- 1 cup pineapple chunks
- 1 orange, peeled and segmented
- 1 mango, peeled and pitted
- 1/2 cup coconut water
- 1 lime, juiced
- Ice cubes (optional)

Optional Add-ins:

- 1 tablespoon honey or agave syrup for added sweetness
- Mint leaves for garnish

Instructions:

Prepare Ingredients:
- Peel and chop the mango, peel and segment the orange, and cut the pineapple into chunks.

Juicing Process:
- In a juicer, combine the pineapple chunks, orange segments, mango chunks, and coconut water.

Add Lime Juice:
- Squeeze the juice of one lime into the juicer. Lime adds a zesty and citrusy flavor to the tropical blend.

Optional Sweetener:
- If you prefer a sweeter juice, you can add honey or agave syrup. Start with a small amount and adjust to your taste.

Mix Well:
- Allow the juicer to process the ingredients, ensuring that all the flavors are well combined.

Strain (Optional):
- If you prefer a smoother juice, you can strain the mixture using a fine mesh sieve or cheesecloth. This step is optional, as some may prefer the added fiber from the fruits.

Chill or Add Ice:
- Refrigerate the juice for a few hours or serve it over ice cubes for a chilled experience.

Garnish (Optional):
- Garnish with mint leaves for a decorative and aromatic touch.

Serve and Enjoy:
- Pour the Tropical Paradise Juice into glasses and enjoy the vibrant and tropical flavors.

This Tropical Paradise Juice is not only delicious but also packed with the goodness of tropical fruits. Feel free to customize the recipe based on your preferences and enjoy a taste of the tropics!

Berry Bliss

Ingredients:

- 1 cup strawberries, hulled
- 1/2 cup blueberries
- 1/2 cup raspberries
- 1 cup blackberries
- 1 tablespoon fresh lemon juice
- 1-2 tablespoons honey or agave syrup (optional)
- 1 cup water or coconut water
- Ice cubes (optional)

Optional Add-ins:

- A handful of mint leaves for added freshness
- Chia seeds for extra fiber and nutrients

Instructions:

Prepare Ingredients:
- Wash the strawberries, blueberries, raspberries, and blackberries thoroughly. Remove the hulls from the strawberries.

Juicing Process:
- In a blender, combine the strawberries, blueberries, raspberries, blackberries, and water (or coconut water).

Add Lemon Juice:
- Squeeze the juice of one fresh lemon into the blender. Lemon juice adds a zesty element to enhance the berry flavors.

Optional Sweetener:
- If you desire a sweeter taste, add honey or agave syrup. Start with a small amount and adjust according to your sweetness preference.

Optional Add-ins:
- For added freshness, include a handful of mint leaves. Additionally, you can add chia seeds for extra texture and nutritional benefits.

Blend until Smooth:
- Blend all the ingredients until you achieve a smooth consistency. If you prefer a colder juice, you can add ice cubes during this step.

Strain (Optional):
- Optionally, strain the juice using a fine mesh sieve or cheesecloth if you prefer a smoother texture. This step is based on personal preference.

Chill or Add Ice:

- Refrigerate the juice for a short time or serve it immediately over ice cubes for a refreshing and chilled experience.

Serve and Enjoy:
- Pour the Berry Bliss Juice into glasses, and savor the delightful flavors of mixed berries.

Feel free to customize this recipe to suit your taste preferences. This Berry Bliss Juice is not only delicious but also rich in antioxidants and vitamins from the assortment of berries. Enjoy!

Carrot Zinger

Ingredients:

- 4 large carrots, peeled and chopped
- 1 orange, peeled and segmented
- 1 apple, cored and sliced
- 1-inch piece of ginger, peeled
- 1 lemon, peeled
- Optional: a pinch of cayenne pepper for an extra zing

Instructions:

Prepare Ingredients:
- Peel and chop the carrots.
- Peel and segment the orange.
- Core and slice the apple.
- Peel the ginger and lemon.

Juicing Process:
- In a juicer, combine the chopped carrots, orange segments, apple slices, peeled ginger, and peeled lemon.

Optional Zing:
- For an extra kick, you can add a pinch of cayenne pepper to the ingredients before juicing.

Juice It:
- Process all the ingredients through the juicer until you get a smooth juice.

Mix Well:
- Stir the juice well to ensure all the flavors are combined.

Strain (Optional):
- If you prefer a smoother juice, you can strain it using a fine mesh sieve or cheesecloth. This step is optional, as some may enjoy the added fiber.

Serve Chilled:
- Refrigerate the juice for a short time or serve it over ice cubes for a refreshing experience.

Garnish (Optional):
- Optionally, garnish with a slice of orange or a sprig of mint for a decorative touch.

Enjoy:
- Pour the Carrot Zinger Juice into glasses and enjoy the invigorating and zesty flavors.

This Carrot Zinger Juice is not only tasty but also loaded with vitamins and nutrients from the carrots, oranges, apples, and ginger. Adjust the quantities based on your taste preferences, and feel free to experiment with the ingredients to suit your liking. Cheers to a healthy and refreshing drink!

Refreshing Cucumber Mint

Ingredients:

- 2 cucumbers, peeled and sliced
- Handful of fresh mint leaves
- 1 lime, peeled
- 1 green apple, cored and sliced
- 1 cup water or coconut water
- Ice cubes (optional)

Optional Add-ins:

- A pinch of salt for enhanced flavor
- Honey or agave syrup for sweetness

Instructions:

Prepare Ingredients:
- Peel and slice the cucumbers.
- Peel the lime.
- Core and slice the green apple.

Juicing Process:
- In a juicer, combine the sliced cucumbers, fresh mint leaves, peeled lime, and sliced green apple.

Optional Add-ins:
- For enhanced flavor, you can add a pinch of salt. If you prefer a sweeter taste, add honey or agave syrup to the juicer.

Juice It:
- Process all the ingredients through the juicer until you achieve a smooth juice.

Mix Well:
- Stir the juice to ensure the minty freshness is evenly distributed.

Strain (Optional):
- If you prefer a smoother juice, you can strain it using a fine mesh sieve or cheesecloth. This step is optional, as some may enjoy the added texture.

Serve Chilled:
- Refrigerate the juice for a short time or serve it over ice cubes for a crisp and refreshing experience.

Garnish (Optional):
- Optionally, garnish with a cucumber slice or a sprig of mint for a decorative touch.

Enjoy:

- Pour the Refreshing Cucumber Mint Juice into glasses and relish the revitalizing and cooling flavors.

This juice is not only hydrating but also carries the invigorating properties of mint. Customize the recipe according to your taste preferences, and enjoy a delicious and revitalizing beverage!

Beetroot Apple Energizer

Ingredients:

- 1 beetroot, peeled and chopped
- 2 apples, cored and sliced
- 1 carrot, peeled and sliced
- 1 lemon, peeled
- 1-inch piece of ginger, peeled
- Optional: a pinch of cinnamon for extra warmth

Instructions:

Prepare Ingredients:
- Peel and chop the beetroot.
- Core and slice the apples.
- Peel the lemon.
- Peel and slice the ginger.
- Peel and slice the carrot.

Juicing Process:
- In a juicer, combine the chopped beetroot, sliced apples, sliced carrot, peeled lemon, and sliced ginger.

Optional Add-ins:
- For an extra layer of flavor, you can add a pinch of cinnamon to the juicer.

Juice It:
- Process all the ingredients through the juicer until you obtain a vibrant and energizing juice.

Mix Well:
- Stir the juice to ensure all the flavors are well combined.

Strain (Optional):
- If you prefer a smoother juice, you can strain it using a fine mesh sieve or cheesecloth. This step is optional.

Serve Chilled:
- Refrigerate the juice for a short time or serve it over ice cubes for a refreshing and invigorating experience.

Garnish (Optional):
- Optionally, you can garnish with a slice of apple or a twist of lemon for a decorative touch.

Enjoy:

- Pour the Beetroot Apple Energizer Juice into glasses and relish the revitalizing and nutrient-packed flavors.

This juice combines the earthy sweetness of beetroot with the crispness of apples and the zesty kick from lemon and ginger, creating a powerful and refreshing drink. Adjust the quantities to suit your taste preferences and enjoy the natural energy boost!

Citrus Carrot Glow

Ingredients:

- 4 large carrots, peeled and chopped
- 2 oranges, peeled and segmented
- 1 grapefruit, peeled and segmented
- 1 lemon, peeled
- 1-inch piece of ginger, peeled
- Optional: a small handful of fresh mint leaves for extra freshness

Instructions:

Prepare Ingredients:
- Peel and chop the carrots.
- Peel and segment the oranges and grapefruit.
- Peel the lemon.
- Peel and slice the ginger.

Juicing Process:
- In a juicer, combine the chopped carrots, segmented oranges, segmented grapefruit, peeled lemon, and sliced ginger.

Optional Add-ins:
- For an extra burst of freshness, you can add a small handful of fresh mint leaves to the juicer.

Juice It:
- Process all the ingredients through the juicer until you achieve a vibrant and glowing juice.

Mix Well:
- Stir the juice to ensure all the flavors are well combined.

Strain (Optional):
- If you prefer a smoother juice, you can strain it using a fine mesh sieve or cheesecloth. This step is optional.

Serve Chilled:
- Refrigerate the juice for a short time or serve it over ice cubes for a refreshing and invigorating experience.

Garnish (Optional):
- Optionally, you can garnish with a slice of orange or a sprig of mint for a decorative touch.

Enjoy:

- Pour the Citrus Carrot Glow Juice into glasses and savor the rejuvenating and nutrient-rich flavors.

This juice combines the sweetness of carrots with the citrusy brightness of oranges, grapefruit, and lemon, creating a refreshing and revitalizing beverage. Customize the recipe according to your taste preferences and enjoy the glow!

Cranberry Orange Refresher

Ingredients:

- 1 cup fresh or unsweetened cranberry juice
- 1 orange, peeled and segmented
- 1/2 lemon, juiced
- 1-2 tablespoons honey or agave syrup (adjust to taste)
- 1 cup cold water
- Ice cubes

Optional Add-ins:

- A splash of sparkling water for effervescence
- Fresh mint leaves for garnish

Instructions:

Prepare Ingredients:
- If using fresh cranberries, juice them to obtain 1 cup of cranberry juice.
- Peel and segment the orange.
- Juice half a lemon.

Combining Ingredients:
- In a blender or mixing pitcher, combine the fresh or unsweetened cranberry juice, orange segments, lemon juice, honey or agave syrup, and cold water.

Optional Sparkle:
- If you enjoy effervescence, add a splash of sparkling water to the mixture. Stir gently to combine.

Adjust Sweetness:
- Taste the mixture and adjust the sweetness by adding more honey or agave syrup if needed.

Chill:
- Refrigerate the mixture for at least 30 minutes to allow the flavors to meld and the drink to chill.

Serve Over Ice:
- When ready to serve, pour the Cranberry Orange Refresher over ice cubes in glasses.

Optional Garnish:
- Garnish with a slice of orange or a few fresh mint leaves for an extra burst of flavor and a decorative touch.

Stir and Enjoy:
- Give the drink a gentle stir before enjoying your Cranberry Orange Refresher.

This refreshing beverage combines the tartness of cranberries with the citrusy brightness of oranges, creating a delightful and thirst-quenching refresher. Feel free to customize the sweetness and add sparkling water for a fizzy kick. Enjoy!

Pomegranate Mint Quencher

Ingredients:

- 1 cup pomegranate seeds
- 1 apple, cored and sliced
- 1/2 cucumber, peeled and sliced
- 1/4 cup fresh mint leaves
- 1 lime, juiced
- 1 tablespoon honey or agave syrup (adjust to taste)
- 1 cup cold water
- Ice cubes

Optional Add-ins:

- A splash of sparkling water for effervescence
- Pomegranate arils and mint leaves for garnish

Instructions:

Prepare Ingredients:
- Extract 1 cup of pomegranate seeds.
- Core and slice the apple.
- Peel and slice the cucumber.
- Juice the lime.

Combining Ingredients:
- In a blender or mixing pitcher, combine the pomegranate seeds, sliced apple, sliced cucumber, fresh mint leaves, lime juice, honey or agave syrup, and cold water.

Optional Sparkle:
- For a fizzy twist, add a splash of sparkling water to the mixture. Gently stir to combine.

Adjust Sweetness:
- Taste the mixture and adjust the sweetness by adding more honey or agave syrup if needed.

Chill:
- Refrigerate the mixture for at least 30 minutes to enhance the flavors and chill the drink.

Serve Over Ice:
- When ready to serve, pour the Pomegranate Mint Quencher Juice over ice cubes in glasses.

Optional Garnish:
- Garnish with a few pomegranate arils and mint leaves for a visually appealing touch.

Stir and Enjoy:
- Give the drink a gentle stir and enjoy the refreshing and hydrating Pomegranate Mint Quencher Juice.

This juice combines the sweet and tart notes of pomegranate with the crispness of apple, the coolness of cucumber, and the invigorating freshness of mint. Customize the sweetness and add sparkling water for an extra bubbly experience. Cheers to a revitalizing drink!

Watermelon Basil Splash

Ingredients:

- 2 cups watermelon cubes, seeds removed
- Handful of fresh basil leaves
- 1 lime, juiced
- 1 tablespoon honey or agave syrup (adjust to taste)
- 1 cup cold water
- Ice cubes

Optional Add-ins:

- A splash of coconut water for added hydration
- Fresh basil leaves for garnish

Instructions:

Prepare Ingredients:
- Cut the watermelon into cubes, ensuring seeds are removed.
- Wash and pat dry the fresh basil leaves.
- Juice the lime.

Blending Process:
- In a blender, combine the watermelon cubes, fresh basil leaves, lime juice, honey or agave syrup, and cold water.

Optional Coconut Water:
- For added hydration and a subtle tropical twist, you can add a splash of coconut water to the mixture.

Blend until Smooth:
- Blend all the ingredients until you achieve a smooth and refreshing consistency.

Adjust Sweetness:
- Taste the mixture and adjust the sweetness by adding more honey or agave syrup if desired.

Chill:
- Refrigerate the mixture for at least 30 minutes to enhance the flavors and chill the drink.

Serve Over Ice:
- When ready to serve, pour the Watermelon Basil Splash over ice cubes in glasses.

Optional Garnish:

- Garnish with a few fresh basil leaves for an extra touch of aroma and presentation.

Stir and Enjoy:
- Give the drink a gentle stir and savor the delightful combination of watermelon and basil in this refreshing splash.

This Watermelon Basil Splash is a perfect hydrating and rejuvenating drink, especially on warm days. Adjust the sweetness and experiment with additional ingredients to suit your taste preferences. Enjoy the burst of summer flavors!

Grapefruit Mint Cooler

Ingredients:

- 2 pink grapefruits, peeled and segmented
- Handful of fresh mint leaves
- 1 lime, juiced
- 1-2 tablespoons honey or agave syrup (adjust to taste)
- 1 cup cold water
- Ice cubes

Optional Add-ins:

- A splash of sparkling water for effervescence
- Grapefruit slices and mint sprigs for garnish

Instructions:

Prepare Ingredients:
- Peel and segment the pink grapefruits.
- Wash and pat dry the fresh mint leaves.
- Juice the lime.

Blending Process:
- In a blender, combine the grapefruit segments, fresh mint leaves, lime juice, honey or agave syrup, and cold water.

Optional Sparkle:
- For a fizzy touch, add a splash of sparkling water to the mixture. Gently stir to combine.

Blend until Smooth:
- Blend all the ingredients until you achieve a smooth and citrusy consistency.

Adjust Sweetness:
- Taste the mixture and adjust the sweetness by adding more honey or agave syrup if desired.

Chill:
- Refrigerate the mixture for at least 30 minutes to let the flavors meld and to chill the Grapefruit Mint Cooler.

Serve Over Ice:
- When ready to serve, pour the Grapefruit Mint Cooler over ice cubes in glasses.

Optional Garnish:
- Garnish with grapefruit slices and mint sprigs for an elegant presentation.

Stir and Enjoy:

- Give the drink a gentle stir and relish the refreshing and minty Grapefruit Mint Cooler.

This cooler combines the tangy goodness of grapefruit with the cooling sensation of mint, creating a revitalizing beverage perfect for hot days. Customize the sweetness and add sparkling water for extra effervescence. Cheers to a delightful and thirst-quenching drink!

Kiwi Lime Splash

Ingredients:

- 4 ripe kiwis, peeled and sliced
- 2 limes, juiced
- 1-2 tablespoons honey or agave syrup (adjust to taste)
- 1 cup cold water
- Ice cubes

Optional Add-ins:

- A splash of coconut water for a tropical twist
- Mint leaves for a burst of freshness

Instructions:

Prepare Ingredients:
- Peel and slice the ripe kiwis.
- Juice the limes.

Blending Process:
- In a blender, combine the sliced kiwis, lime juice, honey or agave syrup, and cold water.

Optional Coconut Water:
- For a tropical twist, you can add a splash of coconut water to the mixture.

Blend until Smooth:
- Blend all the ingredients until you achieve a smooth and vibrant kiwi lime blend.

Adjust Sweetness:
- Taste the mixture and adjust the sweetness by adding more honey or agave syrup if desired.

Chill:
- Refrigerate the mixture for at least 30 minutes to enhance the flavors and chill the Kiwi Lime Splash.

Serve Over Ice:
- When ready to serve, pour the Kiwi Lime Splash over ice cubes in glasses.

Optional Garnish:
- Garnish with mint leaves for an extra burst of freshness.

Stir and Enjoy:
- Give the drink a gentle stir and enjoy the delightful and tangy Kiwi Lime Splash.

This refreshing splash combines the tartness of kiwi with the zesty brightness of lime, creating a perfect balance of flavors. Customize the sweetness and try adding coconut water or mint for additional layers of taste. Cheers to a cool and revitalizing beverage!

Turmeric Pineapple Wellness

Ingredients:

- 1 cup fresh pineapple chunks
- 1 apple, cored and sliced
- 1 inch fresh turmeric root, peeled
- 1 inch fresh ginger root, peeled
- 1 lemon, juiced
- 1-2 tablespoons honey or agave syrup (adjust to taste)
- 1 cup cold water
- Ice cubes

Optional Add-ins:

- A pinch of black pepper to enhance turmeric absorption
- Chia seeds for added texture and nutrition

Instructions:

Prepare Ingredients:
- Cut the fresh pineapple into chunks.
- Core and slice the apple.
- Peel the fresh turmeric and ginger.

Blending Process:
- In a blender, combine the pineapple chunks, sliced apple, fresh turmeric, fresh ginger, lemon juice, honey or agave syrup, and cold water.

Optional Black Pepper:
- For enhanced absorption of turmeric's benefits, you can add a pinch of black pepper to the blender.

Blend until Smooth:
- Blend all the ingredients until you achieve a smooth and vibrant Turmeric Pineapple Wellness Juice.

Adjust Sweetness:
- Taste the mixture and adjust the sweetness by adding more honey or agave syrup if needed.

Chill:
- Refrigerate the juice for at least 30 minutes to allow the flavors to meld and to chill the drink.

Serve Over Ice:
- When ready to serve, pour the Turmeric Pineapple Wellness Juice over ice cubes in glasses.

Optional Add-ins:
- If desired, you can add chia seeds to the juice for added texture and nutritional benefits.

Stir and Enjoy:
- Give the drink a gentle stir and enjoy the wellness-promoting Turmeric Pineapple Juice.

This juice combines the tropical sweetness of pineapple with the anti-inflammatory properties of turmeric and the zing of ginger. Customize the sweetness and feel free to add optional ingredients for additional benefits. Cheers to a healthy and flavorful wellness juice!

Mango Passion Paradise

Ingredients:

- 1 large ripe mango, peeled and diced
- 1 cup passion fruit pulp (about 6-8 passion fruits)
- 1 orange, peeled and segmented
- 1 banana
- 1 cup coconut water
- Ice cubes

Optional Add-ins:

- 1-2 tablespoons honey or agave syrup (adjust to taste)
- Chia seeds for added texture
- Mint leaves for garnish

Instructions:

Prepare Ingredients:
- Peel and dice the ripe mango.
- Cut open the passion fruits and scoop out the pulp.
- Peel and segment the orange.
- Peel the banana.

Blending Process:
- In a blender, combine the diced mango, passion fruit pulp, orange segments, banana, and coconut water.

Optional Sweetener:
- If additional sweetness is desired, you can add honey or agave syrup to the blender. Adjust the sweetness according to your taste.

Optional Add-ins:
- For added texture and nutritional benefits, you can include chia seeds in the blender.

Blend until Smooth:
- Blend all the ingredients until you achieve a smooth and tropical Mango Passion Paradise Juice.

Adjust Consistency:
- If the juice is too thick, you can add more coconut water until it reaches your desired consistency.

Chill:

- Refrigerate the juice for a short time or serve it over ice cubes for a chilled experience.

Garnish (Optional):
- Garnish with mint leaves for a decorative touch.

Stir and Enjoy:
- Give the juice a gentle stir and savor the tropical bliss of Mango Passion Paradise Juice.

This refreshing juice combines the sweetness of mango with the exotic flavor of passion fruit, creating a delightful and tropical drink. Feel free to customize the recipe to suit your taste preferences. Enjoy the paradise in a glass!

Strawberry Basil Bliss

Ingredients:

- 1 cup fresh strawberries, hulled
- Handful of fresh basil leaves
- 1 lime, juiced
- 1-2 tablespoons honey or agave syrup (adjust to taste)
- 1 cup cold water
- Ice cubes

Optional Add-ins:

- A splash of sparkling water for effervescence
- Fresh basil leaves for garnish

Instructions:

Prepare Ingredients:
- Hull the fresh strawberries.
- Wash and pat dry the fresh basil leaves.
- Juice the lime.

Blending Process:
- In a blender, combine the hulled strawberries, fresh basil leaves, lime juice, honey or agave syrup, and cold water.

Optional Sparkle:
- For a fizzy twist, add a splash of sparkling water to the blender. Gently stir to combine.

Blend until Smooth:
- Blend all the ingredients until you achieve a smooth and blissful Strawberry Basil mix.

Adjust Sweetness:
- Taste the mixture and adjust the sweetness by adding more honey or agave syrup if desired.

Chill:
- Refrigerate the mixture for at least 30 minutes to enhance the flavors and chill the Strawberry Basil Bliss.

Serve Over Ice:
- When ready to serve, pour the Strawberry Basil Bliss over ice cubes in glasses.

Optional Garnish:

- Garnish with a few fresh basil leaves for an extra burst of aroma and presentation.

Stir and Enjoy:
- Give the drink a gentle stir and revel in the delightful and refreshing Strawberry Basil Bliss.

This delightful blend combines the sweetness of strawberries with the aromatic notes of fresh basil, creating a harmonious and blissful beverage. Customize the sweetness and add sparkling water for an extra bubbly experience. Cheers to a cool and revitalizing drink!

Blueberry Lemonade Quencher

Ingredients:

- 1 cup blueberries (fresh or frozen)
- 1 lemon, juiced
- 2 tablespoons honey or agave syrup (adjust to taste)
- 1 cup cold water
- Ice cubes

Optional Add-ins:

- A splash of sparkling water for effervescence
- Lemon slices and blueberries for garnish
- Fresh mint leaves for an extra burst of freshness

Instructions:

Prepare Ingredients:
- If using fresh blueberries, rinse them thoroughly. If using frozen blueberries, allow them to thaw slightly.
- Juice the lemon.

Blending Process:
- In a blender, combine the blueberries, lemon juice, honey or agave syrup, and cold water.

Optional Sparkle:
- For a fizzy twist, add a splash of sparkling water to the blender. Gently stir to combine.

Blend until Smooth:
- Blend all the ingredients until you achieve a smooth and quenching Blueberry Lemonade mix.

Adjust Sweetness:
- Taste the mixture and adjust the sweetness by adding more honey or agave syrup if desired.

Chill:
- Refrigerate the mixture for at least 30 minutes to enhance the flavors and chill the Blueberry Lemonade Quencher.

Serve Over Ice:
- When ready to serve, pour the Blueberry Lemonade Quencher over ice cubes in glasses.

Optional Garnish:

- Garnish with lemon slices, blueberries, and fresh mint leaves for an appealing presentation.

Stir and Enjoy:
- Give the drink a gentle stir and enjoy the refreshing and revitalizing Blueberry Lemonade Quencher.

This juice combines the sweet and tart flavors of blueberries with the zesty brightness of lemon, creating a perfect summer quencher. Customize the sweetness, add sparkling water for extra fizz, and garnish for a visually appealing treat. Cheers to a delicious and hydrating drink!

Carrot Pineapple Ginger Zing

Ingredients:

- 4 large carrots, peeled and chopped
- 1 cup fresh pineapple chunks
- 1-inch piece of ginger, peeled
- 1 lemon, juiced
- 1-2 tablespoons honey or agave syrup (adjust to taste)
- 1 cup cold water
- Ice cubes

Optional Add-ins:

- A pinch of cayenne pepper for extra zing
- Fresh mint leaves for garnish

Instructions:

Prepare Ingredients:
- Peel and chop the carrots.
- Cut the fresh pineapple into chunks.
- Peel the ginger.
- Juice the lemon.

Juicing Process:
- In a juicer, combine the chopped carrots, fresh pineapple chunks, peeled ginger, lemon juice, honey or agave syrup, and cold water.

Optional Cayenne Pepper:
- For an extra zing, you can add a pinch of cayenne pepper to the juicer.

Juice It:
- Process all the ingredients through the juicer until you get a smooth and zesty Carrot Pineapple Ginger Zing Juice.

Adjust Sweetness:
- Taste the juice and adjust the sweetness by adding more honey or agave syrup if needed.

Chill:
- Refrigerate the juice for a short time or serve it over ice cubes for a refreshing and zingy experience.

Optional Garnish:
- Garnish with fresh mint leaves for a decorative touch.

Stir and Enjoy:

- Give the juice a gentle stir and enjoy the invigorating and zesty flavors of the Carrot Pineapple Ginger Zing Juice.

This juice combines the sweetness of carrots and pineapple with the spiciness of ginger, creating a zingy and revitalizing beverage. Customize the sweetness, add cayenne pepper for extra kick, and garnish with mint for a refreshing finish. Cheers to a healthy and flavorful drink!

Minty Melon Cooler

Ingredients:

- 2 cups cubed watermelon
- 1 cup cubed honeydew melon
- Handful of fresh mint leaves
- 1 lime, juiced
- 1-2 tablespoons honey or agave syrup (adjust to taste)
- 1 cup cold water
- Ice cubes

Optional Add-ins:

- A splash of coconut water for a tropical twist
- Fresh mint sprigs for garnish

Instructions:

Prepare Ingredients:
- Cube the watermelon and honeydew melon.
- Wash and pat dry the fresh mint leaves.
- Juice the lime.

Blending Process:
- In a blender, combine the cubed watermelon, cubed honeydew melon, fresh mint leaves, lime juice, honey or agave syrup, and cold water.

Optional Coconut Water:
- For a tropical twist, you can add a splash of coconut water to the blender.

Blend until Smooth:
- Blend all the ingredients until you achieve a smooth and minty melon blend.

Adjust Sweetness:
- Taste the mixture and adjust the sweetness by adding more honey or agave syrup if desired.

Chill:
- Refrigerate the mixture for at least 30 minutes to enhance the flavors and chill the Minty Melon Cooler Juice.

Serve Over Ice:
- When ready to serve, pour the Minty Melon Cooler Juice over ice cubes in glasses.

Optional Garnish:

- Garnish with fresh mint sprigs for an extra touch of freshness.

Stir and Enjoy:
- Give the juice a gentle stir and enjoy the cool and minty flavors of the Minty Melon Cooler.

This juice brings together the sweet and hydrating melons with the refreshing essence of mint, creating a perfect cooler for hot days. Customize the sweetness, add coconut water for a tropical vibe, and garnish for a beautiful presentation. Cheers to a revitalizing and minty beverage!

Cucumber Kiwi Refresher

Ingredients:

- 1 cucumber, peeled and sliced
- 3 kiwis, peeled and sliced
- Handful of fresh mint leaves
- 1 lime, juiced
- 1-2 tablespoons honey or agave syrup (adjust to taste)
- 1 cup cold water
- Ice cubes

Optional Add-ins:

- A pinch of salt for enhanced flavor
- Fresh basil leaves for a different herbal note

Instructions:

Prepare Ingredients:
- Peel and slice the cucumber.
- Peel and slice the kiwis.
- Wash and pat dry the fresh mint leaves.
- Juice the lime.

Blending Process:
- In a blender, combine the sliced cucumber, sliced kiwis, fresh mint leaves, lime juice, honey or agave syrup, and cold water.

Optional Salt:
- For enhanced flavor, you can add a pinch of salt to the blender.

Blend until Smooth:
- Blend all the ingredients until you achieve a smooth and refreshing Cucumber Kiwi Refresher Juice.

Adjust Sweetness:
- Taste the mixture and adjust the sweetness by adding more honey or agave syrup if needed.

Chill:
- Refrigerate the mixture for at least 30 minutes to enhance the flavors and chill the juice.

Serve Over Ice:
- When ready to serve, pour the Cucumber Kiwi Refresher Juice over ice cubes in glasses.

Optional Basil Garnish:

- Optionally, garnish with fresh basil leaves for a different herbal note.

Stir and Enjoy:
- Give the juice a gentle stir and enjoy the cool and revitalizing flavors of the Cucumber Kiwi Refresher.

This juice combines the crispness of cucumber with the tropical sweetness of kiwi, creating a hydrating and invigorating beverage. Customize the sweetness, add a pinch of salt for flavor balance, and experiment with basil for a unique twist. Cheers to a refreshing and healthful drink!

Raspberry Peach Paradise

Ingredients:

- 1 cup fresh or frozen raspberries
- 2 ripe peaches, pitted and sliced
- Handful of fresh mint leaves
- 1 lemon, juiced
- 1-2 tablespoons honey or agave syrup (adjust to taste)
- 1 cup cold water
- Ice cubes

Optional Add-ins:

- A splash of coconut water for a tropical touch
- Fresh raspberries and mint sprigs for garnish

Instructions:

Prepare Ingredients:
- If using fresh raspberries, wash them thoroughly. If using frozen raspberries, allow them to thaw slightly.
- Pit and slice the ripe peaches.
- Wash and pat dry the fresh mint leaves.
- Juice the lemon.

Blending Process:
- In a blender, combine the raspberries, sliced peaches, fresh mint leaves, lemon juice, honey or agave syrup, and cold water.

Optional Coconut Water:
- For a tropical twist, you can add a splash of coconut water to the blender.

Blend until Smooth:
- Blend all the ingredients until you achieve a smooth and paradise-worthy Raspberry Peach Juice.

Adjust Sweetness:
- Taste the mixture and adjust the sweetness by adding more honey or agave syrup if desired.

Chill:
- Refrigerate the mixture for at least 30 minutes to enhance the flavors and chill the Raspberry Peach Paradise Juice.

Serve Over Ice:
- When ready to serve, pour the juice over ice cubes in glasses.

Optional Garnish:
- Garnish with a few fresh raspberries and mint sprigs for an extra touch of paradise.

Stir and Enjoy:
- Give the juice a gentle stir and revel in the tropical and fruity goodness of the Raspberry Peach Paradise.

This juice combines the sweetness of ripe peaches with the tartness of raspberries, creating a paradise-inspired beverage. Customize the sweetness, add coconut water for a tropical vibe, and garnish for a visually appealing treat. Cheers to a refreshing and flavorful paradise juice!

Apple Ginger Pear Refresher

Ingredients:

- 2 apples, cored and sliced
- 2 ripe pears, cored and sliced
- 1-inch piece of ginger, peeled
- 1 lemon, juiced
- 1-2 tablespoons honey or agave syrup (adjust to taste)
- 1 cup cold water
- Ice cubes

Optional Add-ins:

- A sprinkle of ground cinnamon for warmth
- Sparkling water for effervescence
- Fresh apple slices or pear wedges for garnish

Instructions:

Prepare Ingredients:
- Core and slice the apples.
- Core and slice the ripe pears.
- Peel the ginger.
- Juice the lemon.

Blending Process:
- In a blender, combine the sliced apples, sliced pears, peeled ginger, lemon juice, honey or agave syrup, and cold water.

Optional Cinnamon:
- For added warmth, you can sprinkle a bit of ground cinnamon into the blender.

Blend until Smooth:
- Blend all the ingredients until you achieve a smooth and refreshing Apple Ginger Pear Refresher.

Adjust Sweetness:
- Taste the mixture and adjust the sweetness by adding more honey or agave syrup if desired.

Chill:
- Refrigerate the mixture for at least 30 minutes to enhance the flavors and chill the refresher.

Serve Over Ice:
- When ready to serve, pour the Apple Ginger Pear Refresher over ice cubes in glasses.

Optional Garnish:
- Garnish with fresh apple slices or pear wedges for an elegant touch.

Stir and Enjoy:
- Give the drink a gentle stir and enjoy the crisp and rejuvenating flavors of the Apple Ginger Pear Refresher.

This juice combines the sweetness of apples and pears with the zing of ginger, creating a refreshing and invigorating beverage. Customize the sweetness, add cinnamon for warmth, and garnish for an extra visual appeal. Cheers to a delightful and healthful refresher!

Cantaloupe Basil Bliss

Ingredients:
- 2 cups cubed cantaloupe
- Handful of fresh basil leaves
- 1 lime, juiced
- 1-2 tablespoons honey or agave syrup (adjust to taste)
- 1 cup cold water
- Ice cubes

Optional Add-ins:
- A splash of coconut water for tropical vibes
- Fresh basil leaves for garnish

Instructions:

Prepare Ingredients:
- Cube the cantaloupe.
- Wash and pat dry the fresh basil leaves.
- Juice the lime.

Blending Process:
- In a blender, combine the cubed cantaloupe, fresh basil leaves, lime juice, honey or agave syrup, and cold water.

Optional Coconut Water:
- For tropical vibes, you can add a splash of coconut water to the blender.

Blend until Smooth:
- Blend all the ingredients until you achieve a smooth and blissful Cantaloupe Basil Bliss Juice.

Adjust Sweetness:

- Taste the mixture and adjust the sweetness by adding more honey or agave syrup if desired.

Chill:
- Refrigerate the mixture for at least 30 minutes to enhance the flavors and chill the juice.

Serve Over Ice:
- When ready to serve, pour the Cantaloupe Basil Bliss Juice over ice cubes in glasses.

Optional Garnish:
- Garnish with fresh basil leaves for an extra burst of aroma and presentation.

Stir and Enjoy:
- Give the juice a gentle stir and revel in the delightful and refreshing Cantaloupe Basil Bliss.

This juice combines the sweet and juicy flavors of cantaloupe with the aromatic essence of fresh basil, creating a blissful and hydrating beverage. Customize the sweetness, add coconut water for a tropical twist, and garnish for an elegant touch. Cheers to a cool and revitalizing drink!

Turmeric Orange Carrot Crush

Ingredients:

- 4 medium-sized carrots, peeled and chopped
- 3 oranges, peeled and segmented
- 1-inch piece of fresh turmeric, peeled
- 1 lemon, juiced
- 1-2 tablespoons honey or agave syrup (adjust to taste)
- 1 cup cold water
- Ice cubes

Optional Add-ins:

- A pinch of black pepper for enhanced turmeric absorption
- Fresh ginger for added warmth
- Orange slices and mint leaves for garnish

Instructions:

Prepare Ingredients:
- Peel and chop the carrots.
- Peel and segment the oranges.
- Peel the fresh turmeric.

Blending Process:
- In a blender, combine the chopped carrots, segmented oranges, peeled turmeric, lemon juice, honey or agave syrup, and cold water.

Optional Black Pepper:
- For enhanced turmeric absorption, you can add a pinch of black pepper to the blender.

Optional Ginger:
- If you enjoy warmth, add a small piece of fresh ginger to the blender.

Blend until Smooth:
- Blend all the ingredients until you achieve a smooth and vibrant Turmeric Orange Carrot Crush.

Adjust Sweetness:
- Taste the mixture and adjust the sweetness by adding more honey or agave syrup if needed.

Chill:
- Refrigerate the mixture for at least 30 minutes to let the flavors meld and to chill the crush.

Serve Over Ice:

- When ready to serve, pour the Turmeric Orange Carrot Crush over ice cubes in glasses.

Optional Garnish:
- Garnish with orange slices and mint leaves for a visually appealing touch.

Stir and Enjoy:
- Give the crush a gentle stir and savor the refreshing and healthful Turmeric Orange Carrot Crush.

This crush combines the earthy notes of turmeric with the sweetness of oranges and carrots, creating a flavorful and nutritious beverage. Customize the sweetness, add optional ingredients for extra warmth, and garnish for a beautiful presentation. Cheers to a vibrant and rejuvenating crush!

Pineapple Mint Cucumber Quencher

Ingredients:

- 2 cups fresh pineapple chunks
- 1 cucumber, peeled and sliced
- Handful of fresh mint leaves
- 1 lime, juiced
- 1-2 tablespoons honey or agave syrup (adjust to taste)
- 1 cup cold water
- Ice cubes

Optional Add-ins:

- A splash of coconut water for a tropical touch
- Fresh cucumber slices and mint sprigs for garnish

Instructions:

Prepare Ingredients:
- Cut the fresh pineapple into chunks.
- Peel and slice the cucumber.
- Wash and pat dry the fresh mint leaves.
- Juice the lime.

Blending Process:
- In a blender, combine the pineapple chunks, sliced cucumber, fresh mint leaves, lime juice, honey or agave syrup, and cold water.

Optional Coconut Water:
- For a tropical touch, you can add a splash of coconut water to the blender.

Blend until Smooth:
- Blend all the ingredients until you achieve a smooth and quenching Pineapple Mint Cucumber Quencher Juice.

Adjust Sweetness:
- Taste the mixture and adjust the sweetness by adding more honey or agave syrup if desired.

Chill:
- Refrigerate the mixture for at least 30 minutes to enhance the flavors and chill the juice.

Serve Over Ice:
- When ready to serve, pour the Pineapple Mint Cucumber Quencher Juice over ice cubes in glasses.

Optional Garnish:

- Garnish with fresh cucumber slices and mint sprigs for a refreshing and visually appealing touch.

Stir and Enjoy:
- Give the juice a gentle stir and revel in the tropical and hydrating flavors of the Pineapple Mint Cucumber Quencher.

This juice combines the sweetness of pineapple with the crispness of cucumber and the freshness of mint, creating a perfect quencher for hot days. Customize the sweetness, add coconut water for a tropical twist, and garnish for an extra visual delight. Cheers to a cool and revitalizing beverage!

Strawberry Kiwi Kale Kick

Ingredients:

- 1 cup fresh strawberries, hulled
- 2 ripe kiwis, peeled and sliced
- Handful of fresh kale leaves, stems removed
- 1 lime, juiced
- 1-2 tablespoons honey or agave syrup (adjust to taste)
- 1 cup cold water
- Ice cubes

Optional Add-ins:

- A small piece of ginger for a hint of warmth
- Chia seeds for added texture and nutrition

Instructions:

Prepare Ingredients:
- Hull the fresh strawberries.
- Peel and slice the ripe kiwis.
- Remove the stems from the fresh kale leaves.
- Juice the lime.

Blending Process:
- In a blender, combine the hulled strawberries, sliced kiwis, fresh kale leaves, lime juice, honey or agave syrup, and cold water.

Optional Ginger:
- For a hint of warmth, you can add a small piece of peeled ginger to the blender.

Optional Chia Seeds:
- If desired, you can add chia seeds to the blender for added texture and nutritional benefits.

Blend until Smooth:
- Blend all the ingredients until you achieve a smooth and invigorating Strawberry Kiwi Kale Kick.

Adjust Sweetness:
- Taste the mixture and adjust the sweetness by adding more honey or agave syrup if needed.

Chill:

- Refrigerate the mixture for at least 30 minutes to let the flavors meld and to chill the juice.

Serve Over Ice:
- When ready to serve, pour the Strawberry Kiwi Kale Kick over ice cubes in glasses.

Optional Garnish:
- Garnish with a slice of kiwi or a strawberry on the rim of the glass.

Stir and Enjoy:
- Give the juice a gentle stir and enjoy the refreshing and nutrient-packed Strawberry Kiwi Kale Kick.

This juice combines the sweetness of strawberries and kiwis with the nutritional benefits of kale, creating a vibrant and healthful beverage. Customize the sweetness, add ginger for warmth, and experiment with chia seeds for extra nutrition. Cheers to a delicious and energizing drink!

Pear Berry Citrus Splash

Ingredients:

- 2 ripe pears, cored and sliced
- 1 cup mixed berries (such as blueberries, raspberries, or blackberries)
- 1 orange, peeled and segmented
- 1 lemon, juiced
- 1-2 tablespoons honey or agave syrup (adjust to taste)
- 1 cup cold water
- Ice cubes

Optional Add-ins:

- A splash of pomegranate juice for added depth
- Fresh mint leaves for garnish

Instructions:

Prepare Ingredients:
- Core and slice the ripe pears.
- Rinse the mixed berries.
- Peel and segment the orange.
- Juice the lemon.

Blending Process:
- In a blender, combine the sliced pears, mixed berries, orange segments, lemon juice, honey or agave syrup, and cold water.

Optional Pomegranate Juice:
- For added depth, you can add a splash of pomegranate juice to the blender.

Blend until Smooth:
- Blend all the ingredients until you achieve a smooth and refreshing Pear Berry Citrus Splash Juice.

Adjust Sweetness:
- Taste the mixture and adjust the sweetness by adding more honey or agave syrup if desired.

Chill:
- Refrigerate the mixture for at least 30 minutes to enhance the flavors and chill the juice.

Serve Over Ice:

- When ready to serve, pour the Pear Berry Citrus Splash Juice over ice cubes in glasses.

Optional Garnish:
- Garnish with fresh mint leaves for a burst of freshness.

Stir and Enjoy:
- Give the juice a gentle stir and savor the delightful and fruity flavors of the Pear Berry Citrus Splash.

This juice combines the sweetness of pears, the vibrant colors of mixed berries, and the citrusy goodness of orange and lemon, creating a refreshing and hydrating beverage. Customize the sweetness, add pomegranate juice for depth, and garnish with mint for an extra touch. Cheers to a delicious and colorful splash!

Cucumber Pineapple Mint Delight

Ingredients:

- 1 cucumber, peeled and sliced
- 2 cups fresh pineapple chunks
- Handful of fresh mint leaves
- 1 lime, juiced
- 1-2 tablespoons honey or agave syrup (adjust to taste)
- 1 cup cold water
- Ice cubes

Optional Add-ins:

- A splash of coconut water for a tropical twist
- Fresh cucumber slices and mint sprigs for garnish

Instructions:

Prepare Ingredients:
- Peel and slice the cucumber.
- Cut the fresh pineapple into chunks.
- Wash and pat dry the fresh mint leaves.
- Juice the lime.

Blending Process:
- In a blender, combine the sliced cucumber, fresh pineapple chunks, mint leaves, lime juice, honey or agave syrup, and cold water.

Optional Coconut Water:
- For a tropical twist, you can add a splash of coconut water to the blender.

Blend until Smooth:
- Blend all the ingredients until you achieve a smooth and delightful Cucumber Pineapple Mint Juice.

Adjust Sweetness:
- Taste the mixture and adjust the sweetness by adding more honey or agave syrup if needed.

Chill:
- Refrigerate the mixture for at least 30 minutes to enhance the flavors and chill the juice.

Serve Over Ice:
- When ready to serve, pour the Cucumber Pineapple Mint Delight Juice over ice cubes in glasses.

Optional Garnish:
- Garnish with fresh cucumber slices and mint sprigs for a refreshing and visually appealing touch.

Stir and Enjoy:
- Give the juice a gentle stir and enjoy the cool and delightful flavors of the Cucumber Pineapple Mint Delight.

This juice combines the hydrating properties of cucumber, the tropical sweetness of pineapple, and the refreshing essence of mint, creating a delightful and revitalizing beverage. Customize the sweetness, add coconut water for a tropical twist, and garnish for an extra visual appeal. Cheers to a cool and rejuvenating drink!

Blueberry Lavender Lemonade

Ingredients:

- 1 cup fresh or frozen blueberries
- 1 tablespoon dried culinary lavender (or 2-3 fresh lavender sprigs)
- 4 lemons, juiced
- 2-3 tablespoons honey or agave syrup (adjust to taste)
- 1 cup cold water
- Ice cubes

Optional Add-ins:

- A splash of sparkling water for effervescence
- Fresh blueberries and lavender sprigs for garnish

Instructions:

Prepare Ingredients:
- If using fresh blueberries, wash them thoroughly. If using dried lavender, ensure it's culinary-grade. If using fresh lavender, wash the sprigs.
- Juice the lemons.

Infusing Lavender:
- In a small pot, combine the lavender with 1/2 cup of water. Bring to a gentle simmer, then remove from heat and let it steep for about 10 minutes. Strain the lavender, allowing the infused water to cool.

Blending Process:
- In a blender, combine the blueberries, strained lavender-infused water, lemon juice, honey or agave syrup, and cold water.

Optional Sparkle:
- For effervescence, add a splash of sparkling water to the blender.

Blend until Smooth:
- Blend all the ingredients until you achieve a smooth and aromatic Blueberry Lavender Lemonade.

Adjust Sweetness:
- Taste the mixture and adjust the sweetness by adding more honey or agave syrup if needed.

Chill:
- Refrigerate the mixture for at least 30 minutes to enhance the flavors and chill the juice.

Serve Over Ice:

- When ready to serve, pour the Blueberry Lavender Lemonade over ice cubes in glasses.

Optional Garnish:
- Garnish with a few fresh blueberries and lavender sprigs for an elegant touch.

Stir and Enjoy:
- Give the juice a gentle stir and savor the unique and floral notes of the Blueberry Lavender Lemonade.

This juice combines the sweetness of blueberries, the citrusy zing of lemons, and the aromatic touch of lavender, creating a refreshing and sophisticated beverage. Customize the sweetness, add sparkling water for effervescence, and garnish for a visually appealing treat. Cheers to a delightful and aromatic drink!

Gingered Watermelon Lime Quencher

Ingredients:

- 4 cups cubed seedless watermelon
- 1-2 tablespoons fresh ginger, grated
- 2 limes, juiced
- 1-2 tablespoons honey or agave syrup (adjust to taste)
- 1 cup cold water
- Ice cubes

Optional Add-ins:

- A pinch of cayenne pepper for a spicy kick
- Fresh mint leaves for a refreshing twist

Instructions:

Prepare Ingredients:
- Cube the seedless watermelon.
- Grate fresh ginger.
- Juice the limes.

Blending Process:
- In a blender, combine the cubed watermelon, grated ginger, lime juice, honey or agave syrup, and cold water.

Optional Cayenne Pepper:
- For a spicy kick, you can add a pinch of cayenne pepper to the blender.

Blend until Smooth:
- Blend all the ingredients until you achieve a smooth and ginger-infused Watermelon Lime Quencher.

Adjust Sweetness:
- Taste the mixture and adjust the sweetness by adding more honey or agave syrup if needed.

Chill:
- Refrigerate the mixture for at least 30 minutes to enhance the flavors and chill the quencher.

Serve Over Ice:
- When ready to serve, pour the Gingered Watermelon Lime Quencher over ice cubes in glasses.

Optional Mint Garnish:
- Garnish with fresh mint leaves for an extra burst of freshness.

Stir and Enjoy:
- Give the quencher a gentle stir and enjoy the cool and ginger-infused flavors of the Gingered Watermelon Lime Quencher.

This refreshing drink combines the hydrating properties of watermelon with the zing of lime and the warmth of ginger, creating a perfect quencher for hot days. Customize the sweetness, add cayenne pepper for a spicy kick, and garnish with mint for an extra refreshing touch. Cheers to a revitalizing and flavorful beverage!

Mango Basil Beet Boost

Ingredients:

- 2 ripe mangoes, peeled and diced
- Handful of fresh basil leaves
- 1 small beet, peeled and diced
- 1 lime, juiced
- 1-2 tablespoons honey or agave syrup (adjust to taste)
- 1 cup cold water
- Ice cubes

Optional Add-ins:

- A pinch of sea salt for flavor enhancement
- Fresh basil sprigs for garnish

Instructions:

Prepare Ingredients:
- Peel and dice the ripe mangoes.
- Wash and pat dry the fresh basil leaves.
- Peel and dice the small beet.
- Juice the lime.

Blending Process:
- In a blender, combine the diced mangoes, fresh basil leaves, diced beet, lime juice, honey or agave syrup, and cold water.

Optional Sea Salt:
- For flavor enhancement, you can add a pinch of sea salt to the blender.

Blend until Smooth:
- Blend all the ingredients until you achieve a smooth and vibrant Mango Basil Beet Boost.

Adjust Sweetness:
- Taste the mixture and adjust the sweetness by adding more honey or agave syrup if needed.

Chill:
- Refrigerate the mixture for at least 30 minutes to enhance the flavors and chill the boost.

Serve Over Ice:
- When ready to serve, pour the Mango Basil Beet Boost over ice cubes in glasses.

Optional Garnish:
- Garnish with fresh basil sprigs for an elegant touch.

Stir and Enjoy:
- Give the boost a gentle stir and savor the unique and nutritious flavors of the Mango Basil Beet Boost.

This boost combines the tropical sweetness of mangoes with the earthy tones of beets and the aromatic freshness of basil, creating a nutrient-packed and refreshing beverage. Customize the sweetness, add sea salt for flavor balance, and garnish for an extra visual appeal. Cheers to a vibrant and healthful drink!

Smoothie Recipes:

Berry Blast

Ingredients:

- 1 cup mixed berries (strawberries, blueberries, raspberries, blackberries)
- 1 banana, peeled and sliced
- 1/2 cup Greek yogurt (or your favorite yogurt)
- 1/2 cup almond milk (or any milk of your choice)
- 1 tablespoon honey or maple syrup (optional, for added sweetness)
- Ice cubes

Optional Add-ins:

- 1 tablespoon chia seeds or flaxseeds for added nutrition
- Handful of spinach for a green boost
- Protein powder for an extra protein kick

Instructions:

Prepare Ingredients:
- If using fresh berries, wash them thoroughly.
- Peel and slice the banana.

Blending Process:
- In a blender, combine the mixed berries, sliced banana, Greek yogurt, almond milk, and honey (if using).

Optional Add-ins:
- If desired, add chia seeds or flaxseeds for added nutrition, a handful of spinach for a green boost, or protein powder for extra protein.

Blend until Smooth:
- Blend all the ingredients until you achieve a smooth and creamy Berry Blast Smoothie.

Adjust Sweetness:
- Taste the smoothie and adjust the sweetness by adding more honey or maple syrup if needed.

Optional Ice:
- Add ice cubes to the blender and blend again for a chilled and frosty texture.

Serve:
- Pour the Berry Blast Smoothie into a glass.

Optional Garnish:

- Garnish with a few whole berries on top for a decorative touch.

Enjoy:
- Sip and enjoy the refreshing and fruity goodness of the Berry Blast Smoothie!

Feel free to customize the recipe to suit your taste preferences. This smoothie is not only delicious but also packed with vitamins, antioxidants, and natural sweetness from the berries. Cheers to a berry-filled and nutritious treat!

Mango Tango

Ingredients:

- 1 cup frozen mango chunks
- 1 banana, peeled and sliced
- 1/2 cup plain or Greek yogurt
- 1/2 cup orange juice
- 1/2 cup coconut water (or regular water)
- 1 tablespoon honey or agave syrup (optional, for added sweetness)
- Ice cubes

Optional Add-ins:

- A handful of spinach for a nutrient boost
- Chia seeds or flaxseeds for added texture and nutrition
- Coconut flakes for a tropical touch

Instructions:

Prepare Ingredients:
- If not using pre-frozen mango chunks, peel and dice fresh mango and freeze for a few hours.
- Peel and slice the banana.

Blending Process:
- In a blender, combine the frozen mango chunks, sliced banana, yogurt, orange juice, coconut water, and honey (if using).

Optional Add-ins:
- If desired, add a handful of spinach for a nutrient boost, chia seeds or flaxseeds for added texture and nutrition, or coconut flakes for a tropical touch.

Blend until Smooth:
- Blend all the ingredients until you achieve a smooth and creamy Mango Tango Smoothie.

Adjust Sweetness:
- Taste the smoothie and adjust the sweetness by adding more honey or agave syrup if needed.

Optional Ice:
- Add ice cubes to the blender and blend again for a chilled and refreshing texture.

Serve:
- Pour the Mango Tango Smoothie into a glass.

Optional Garnish:

- Garnish with a slice of fresh mango or a sprinkle of coconut flakes for an extra touch.

Enjoy:
- Sip and enjoy the tropical and tangy flavors of the Mango Tango Smoothie!

Feel free to customize the recipe to suit your preferences. This smoothie is not only delicious but also a great source of vitamins, fiber, and hydration. Whether you're looking for a quick breakfast option or a refreshing snack, the Mango Tango Smoothie is sure to delight your taste buds. Cheers to a tropical dance of flavors!

Green Power

Ingredients:

- 1 cup spinach leaves, washed
- 1/2 cucumber, peeled and sliced
- 1/2 avocado, peeled and pitted
- 1/2 green apple, cored and sliced
- 1 tablespoon chia seeds
- 1 tablespoon flaxseeds
- 1/2 lemon, juiced
- 1 cup coconut water (or water)
- Ice cubes

Optional Add-ins:

- Fresh mint leaves for added freshness
- A scoop of protein powder for extra protein
- Banana for added creaminess

Instructions:

Prepare Ingredients:
- Wash the spinach leaves.
- Peel and slice the cucumber.
- Peel and pit the avocado.
- Core and slice the green apple.
- Juice the lemon.

Blending Process:
- In a blender, combine the spinach leaves, sliced cucumber, avocado, green apple, chia seeds, flaxseeds, lemon juice, and coconut water.

Optional Add-ins:
- If desired, add fresh mint leaves for added freshness, a scoop of protein powder for extra protein, or a banana for added creaminess.

Blend until Smooth:
- Blend all the ingredients until you achieve a smooth and vibrant Green Power Smoothie.

Adjust Thickness:
- If the smoothie is too thick, you can add more coconut water or water until you reach your desired consistency.

Optional Ice:
- Add ice cubes to the blender and blend again for a chilled and refreshing texture.

Serve:
- Pour the Green Power Smoothie into a glass.

Optional Garnish:
- Garnish with a few chia seeds or a slice of cucumber for an extra touch.

Enjoy:
- Sip and enjoy the nutrient-packed and energizing Green Power Smoothie!

This smoothie is loaded with greens, fruits, and seeds, providing a boost of vitamins, minerals, and healthy fats. Customize the recipe to suit your taste preferences and dietary needs. Whether you're starting your day or need a midday pick-me-up, this Green Power Smoothie is a delicious and nutritious choice. Cheers to a green and powerful blend!

Chocolate Peanut Butter Delight

Ingredients:

- 1 banana, peeled and sliced
- 2 tablespoons peanut butter (preferably natural)
- 1 tablespoon cocoa powder
- 1 cup unsweetened almond milk (or any milk of your choice)
- 1 tablespoon honey or maple syrup (optional, for added sweetness)
- 1/2 teaspoon vanilla extract
- Ice cubes

Optional Add-ins:

- A scoop of chocolate protein powder for extra protein
- Greek yogurt for added creaminess
- A handful of spinach for a nutrient boost

Instructions:

Prepare Ingredients:
- Peel and slice the banana.

Blending Process:
- In a blender, combine the sliced banana, peanut butter, cocoa powder, almond milk, honey or maple syrup (if using), and vanilla extract.

Optional Add-ins:
- If desired, add a scoop of chocolate protein powder for extra protein, Greek yogurt for added creaminess, or a handful of spinach for a nutrient boost.

Blend until Smooth:
- Blend all the ingredients until you achieve a smooth and luscious Chocolate Peanut Butter Delight Smoothie.

Adjust Sweetness:
- Taste the smoothie and adjust the sweetness by adding more honey or maple syrup if needed.

Optional Ice:
- Add ice cubes to the blender and blend again for a chilled and frosty texture.

Serve:
- Pour the Chocolate Peanut Butter Delight Smoothie into a glass.

Optional Garnish:

- Garnish with a sprinkle of cocoa powder or a few crushed peanuts for an extra indulgent touch.

Enjoy:
- Sip and indulge in the rich and delightful flavors of the Chocolate Peanut Butter Delight Smoothie!

Feel free to customize the recipe based on your preferences. This smoothie combines the classic combination of chocolate and peanut butter for a satisfying and delicious treat. Whether it's a post-workout refuel or a sweet tooth craving, this smoothie is sure to hit the spot. Cheers to a delightful and indulgent blend!

Pineapple Coconut Bliss

Ingredients:

- 1 cup fresh pineapple chunks
- 1/2 cup coconut milk
- 1/2 cup Greek yogurt (or coconut yogurt for a dairy-free option)
- 1 banana, peeled and sliced
- 1 tablespoon shredded coconut (unsweetened)
- 1 tablespoon honey or agave syrup (optional, for added sweetness)
- 1/2 teaspoon vanilla extract
- Ice cubes

Optional Add-ins:

- A squeeze of lime juice for a citrusy twist
- Chia seeds for added texture and nutrition
- Coconut flakes for garnish

Instructions:

Prepare Ingredients:
- Cut fresh pineapple into chunks.
- Peel and slice the banana.

Blending Process:
- In a blender, combine the fresh pineapple chunks, coconut milk, Greek yogurt, sliced banana, shredded coconut, honey or agave syrup (if using), and vanilla extract.

Optional Add-ins:
- For a citrusy twist, add a squeeze of lime juice to the blender. If desired, incorporate chia seeds for added texture and nutrition.

Blend until Smooth:
- Blend all the ingredients until you achieve a smooth and tropical Pineapple Coconut Bliss Smoothie.

Adjust Sweetness:
- Taste the smoothie and adjust the sweetness by adding more honey or agave syrup if needed.

Optional Ice:
- Add ice cubes to the blender and blend again for a chilled and frosty texture.

Serve:
- Pour the Pineapple Coconut Bliss Smoothie into a glass.

Optional Garnish:

- Garnish with a sprinkle of coconut flakes for an extra tropical touch.

Enjoy:
- Sip and bask in the tropical bliss of the Pineapple Coconut Bliss Smoothie!

Feel free to customize the recipe to your liking. This smoothie combines the sweet and tart flavors of pineapple with the creamy richness of coconut for a delightful and refreshing drink. Whether it's a morning pick-me-up or an afternoon treat, this smoothie is sure to transport you to a tropical paradise. Cheers to a blissful and tropical blend!

Blueberry Almond Bliss

Ingredients:

- 1 cup fresh or frozen blueberries
- 1 banana, peeled and sliced
- 1/2 cup almond milk
- 1/4 cup plain Greek yogurt (or almond milk yogurt for a dairy-free option)
- 1 tablespoon almond butter
- 1 tablespoon honey or maple syrup (optional, for added sweetness)
- 1/2 teaspoon almond extract
- Ice cubes

Optional Add-ins:

- A handful of spinach for added nutrients
- Chia seeds for extra texture and nutrition
- Almond slices for garnish

Instructions:

Prepare Ingredients:
- If using fresh blueberries, wash them thoroughly.
- Peel and slice the banana.

Blending Process:
- In a blender, combine the blueberries, sliced banana, almond milk, Greek yogurt, almond butter, honey or maple syrup (if using), and almond extract.

Optional Add-ins:
- For added nutrients, you can include a handful of spinach. If desired, add chia seeds for extra texture and nutrition.

Blend until Smooth:
- Blend all the ingredients until you achieve a smooth and luscious Blueberry Almond Bliss Smoothie.

Adjust Sweetness:
- Taste the smoothie and adjust the sweetness by adding more honey or maple syrup if needed.

Optional Ice:
- Add ice cubes to the blender and blend again for a chilled and refreshing texture.

Serve:
- Pour the Blueberry Almond Bliss Smoothie into a glass.

Optional Garnish:
- Garnish with almond slices for an extra crunch.

Enjoy:
- Sip and indulge in the delicious combination of blueberries and almonds with the Blueberry Almond Bliss Smoothie!

Feel free to modify the recipe according to your preferences. This smoothie offers a perfect balance of sweetness from blueberries, creaminess from almond butter, and the nutty flavor of almond extract. Whether you're starting your day or seeking a tasty snack, this Blueberry Almond Bliss Smoothie is a delightful choice. Cheers to a blissful and nutritious blend!

Cherry Vanilla Dream

Ingredients:

- 1 cup frozen or fresh cherries, pitted
- 1/2 cup vanilla-flavored Greek yogurt (or non-dairy vanilla yogurt)
- 1/2 cup almond milk (or any milk of your choice)
- 1 tablespoon honey or maple syrup (optional, for added sweetness)
- 1/2 teaspoon vanilla extract
- Ice cubes

Optional Add-ins:

- A small handful of rolled oats for added fiber
- Chia seeds for extra texture and nutrition
- A dash of cinnamon for warmth

Instructions:

Prepare Ingredients:
- If using fresh cherries, pit them.

Blending Process:
- In a blender, combine the cherries, vanilla-flavored Greek yogurt, almond milk, honey or maple syrup (if using), and vanilla extract.

Optional Add-ins:
- For added fiber, you can include a small handful of rolled oats. If desired, add chia seeds for extra texture and nutrition. A dash of cinnamon can add warmth to the flavor.

Blend until Smooth:
- Blend all the ingredients until you achieve a smooth and dreamy Cherry Vanilla Dream Smoothie.

Adjust Sweetness:
- Taste the smoothie and adjust the sweetness by adding more honey or maple syrup if needed.

Optional Ice:
- Add ice cubes to the blender and blend again for a chilled and refreshing texture.

Serve:
- Pour the Cherry Vanilla Dream Smoothie into a glass.

Optional Garnish:

- Garnish with a few whole cherries or a sprinkle of chia seeds for an extra touch.

Enjoy:
- Sip and enjoy the delightful combination of cherries and vanilla in the Cherry Vanilla Dream Smoothie!

Feel free to customize the recipe to suit your taste preferences. This smoothie is a sweet and creamy treat with the luscious flavor of cherries and the comforting essence of vanilla. Whether it's breakfast, a snack, or a dessert, the Cherry Vanilla Dream Smoothie is sure to satisfy your cravings. Cheers to a dreamy and delicious blend!

Spinach Pineapple Protein

Ingredients:

- 1 cup fresh spinach leaves, washed
- 1 cup fresh or frozen pineapple chunks
- 1/2 banana, peeled and sliced
- 1/2 cup Greek yogurt (or any yogurt of your choice)
- 1 scoop vanilla protein powder
- 1 tablespoon chia seeds
- 1 cup coconut water (or water)
- Ice cubes

Optional Add-ins:

- A splash of lime juice for a citrusy kick
- A handful of mint leaves for freshness
- Flaxseeds for added Omega-3s

Instructions:

> Prepare Ingredients:
> - Wash the spinach leaves.
> - Peel and slice the banana.
>
> Blending Process:
> - In a blender, combine the fresh spinach leaves, pineapple chunks, sliced banana, Greek yogurt, vanilla protein powder, chia seeds, and coconut water.
>
> Optional Add-ins:
> - For a citrusy kick, add a splash of lime juice. If desired, include a handful of mint leaves for freshness or flaxseeds for added Omega-3s.
>
> Blend until Smooth:
> - Blend all the ingredients until you achieve a smooth and nutritious Spinach Pineapple Protein Smoothie.
>
> Adjust Sweetness:
> - Taste the smoothie and adjust the sweetness by adding more banana or a drizzle of honey if needed.
>
> Optional Ice:
> - Add ice cubes to the blender and blend again for a chilled and refreshing texture.
>
> Serve:

- Pour the Spinach Pineapple Protein Smoothie into a glass.

Optional Garnish:
- Garnish with a pineapple slice or a sprinkle of chia seeds for an extra touch.

Enjoy:
- Sip and relish the protein-packed goodness of the Spinach Pineapple Protein Smoothie!

This smoothie combines the sweetness of pineapple with the nutritional powerhouse of spinach and the protein boost from Greek yogurt and protein powder. Customize the recipe with optional add-ins to suit your taste and nutritional preferences. Whether it's for a post-workout recovery or a nutritious breakfast, this smoothie is a delicious and satisfying choice. Cheers to a vibrant and protein-rich blend!

Mint Chocolate Chip Delight

Ingredients:

- 1 banana, peeled and sliced
- 1 cup fresh spinach leaves, washed
- 1/2 cup fresh mint leaves, packed
- 1 cup almond milk (or any milk of your choice)
- 1 tablespoon cocoa powder
- 1 tablespoon chocolate chips (dark chocolate or semi-sweet)
- 1 tablespoon honey or maple syrup (optional, for added sweetness)
- 1/2 teaspoon peppermint extract
- Ice cubes

Optional Add-ins:

- A scoop of chocolate protein powder for extra protein
- Chia seeds for added texture and nutrition
- Greek yogurt for added creaminess

Instructions:

Prepare Ingredients:
- Peel and slice the banana.
- Wash the spinach and mint leaves.

Blending Process:
- In a blender, combine the sliced banana, fresh spinach leaves, fresh mint leaves, almond milk, cocoa powder, chocolate chips, honey or maple syrup (if using), and peppermint extract.

Optional Add-ins:
- For extra protein, you can add a scoop of chocolate protein powder. If desired, include chia seeds for added texture and nutrition or Greek yogurt for added creaminess.

Blend until Smooth:
- Blend all the ingredients until you achieve a smooth and indulgent Mint Chocolate Chip Delight Smoothie.

Adjust Sweetness:
- Taste the smoothie and adjust the sweetness by adding more honey or maple syrup if needed.

Optional Ice:
- Add ice cubes to the blender and blend again for a chilled and frosty texture.

Serve:

- Pour the Mint Chocolate Chip Delight Smoothie into a glass.

Optional Garnish:
- Garnish with a sprinkle of chocolate chips or a mint leaf for an extra delightful touch.

Enjoy:
- Sip and savor the delightful combination of mint and chocolate in the Mint Chocolate Chip Delight Smoothie!

Feel free to customize the recipe based on your preferences. This smoothie offers a refreshing minty flavor combined with the rich and chocolaty goodness of chocolate chips. Whether it's a special treat or a way to satisfy your chocolate cravings, this Mint Chocolate Chip Delight Smoothie is sure to be a hit. Cheers to a minty and chocolaty blend!

Peachy Green

Ingredients:

- 1 cup frozen or fresh peaches, sliced
- 1 cup fresh spinach leaves, washed
- 1/2 banana, peeled and sliced
- 1/2 cup plain Greek yogurt (or any yogurt of your choice)
- 1/2 cup coconut water (or water)
- 1 tablespoon chia seeds
- 1 tablespoon honey or agave syrup (optional, for added sweetness)
- Ice cubes

Optional Add-ins:

- A splash of lime juice for a citrusy kick
- A handful of mint leaves for freshness
- Flaxseeds for added Omega-3s

Instructions:

Prepare Ingredients:
- If using fresh peaches, slice them.
- Wash the spinach leaves.
- Peel and slice the banana.

Blending Process:
- In a blender, combine the sliced peaches, fresh spinach leaves, sliced banana, Greek yogurt, coconut water, chia seeds, and honey or agave syrup (if using).

Optional Add-ins:
- For a citrusy kick, add a splash of lime juice. If desired, include a handful of mint leaves for freshness or flaxseeds for added Omega-3s.

Blend until Smooth:
- Blend all the ingredients until you achieve a smooth and peachy-green delight.

Adjust Sweetness:
- Taste the smoothie and adjust the sweetness by adding more honey or agave syrup if needed.

Optional Ice:
- Add ice cubes to the blender and blend again for a chilled and refreshing texture.

Serve:
- Pour the Peachy Green Smoothie into a glass.

Optional Garnish:
- Garnish with a slice of peach or a sprinkle of chia seeds for an extra touch.

Enjoy:
- Sip and enjoy the refreshing and peachy goodness of the Peachy Green Smoothie!

Feel free to customize the recipe based on your taste preferences. This smoothie combines the sweetness of peaches with the nutrient-packed freshness of spinach, creating a delightful and healthy drink. Whether it's for breakfast, a snack, or a post-workout refuel, the Peachy Green Smoothie is a delicious choice. Cheers to a peachy and green blend!

Raspberry Almond Protein

Ingredients:

- 1 cup frozen or fresh raspberries
- 1 banana, peeled and sliced
- 1/2 cup almond milk (or any milk of your choice)
- 1/2 cup Greek yogurt (or almond milk yogurt for a dairy-free option)
- 1 scoop vanilla protein powder
- 1 tablespoon almond butter
- 1 tablespoon honey or agave syrup (optional, for added sweetness)
- Ice cubes

Optional Add-ins:

- A handful of spinach for added nutrients
- Chia seeds for extra texture and nutrition
- Almond slices for garnish

Instructions:

- Prepare Ingredients:
    - If using fresh raspberries, wash them thoroughly.
    - Peel and slice the banana.
- Blending Process:
    - In a blender, combine the raspberries, sliced banana, almond milk, Greek yogurt, vanilla protein powder, almond butter, and honey or agave syrup (if using).
- Optional Add-ins:
    - For added nutrients, you can include a handful of spinach. If desired, add chia seeds for extra texture and nutrition.
- Blend until Smooth:
    - Blend all the ingredients until you achieve a smooth and protein-packed Raspberry Almond Protein Smoothie.
- Adjust Sweetness:
    - Taste the smoothie and adjust the sweetness by adding more honey or agave syrup if needed.
- Optional Ice:
    - Add ice cubes to the blender and blend again for a chilled and refreshing texture.
- Serve:

- Pour the Raspberry Almond Protein Smoothie into a glass.

Optional Garnish:
- Garnish with a few fresh raspberries or a sprinkle of almond slices for an extra visual appeal.

Enjoy:
- Sip and relish the delicious combination of raspberries and almonds in the Raspberry Almond Protein Smoothie!

Feel free to customize the recipe to suit your preferences. This smoothie provides a burst of fruity flavor from raspberries, combined with the creamy richness of almond butter and the protein boost from Greek yogurt and protein powder. Whether it's a post-workout recovery or a satisfying breakfast, this Raspberry Almond Protein Smoothie is a nutritious and tasty choice. Cheers to a delicious and protein-rich blend!

Vanilla Berry Delight

Ingredients:

- 1 cup mixed berries (strawberries, blueberries, raspberries, blackberries)
- 1/2 banana, peeled and sliced
- 1/2 cup vanilla-flavored Greek yogurt (or any yogurt of your choice)
- 1/2 cup almond milk (or any milk of your choice)
- 1 teaspoon vanilla extract
- 1 tablespoon honey or agave syrup (optional, for added sweetness)
- Ice cubes

Optional Add-ins:

- A handful of spinach for added nutrients
- Chia seeds for extra texture and nutrition
- Granola for a crunchy topping

Instructions:

   Prepare Ingredients:
   - If using fresh berries, wash them thoroughly.
   - Peel and slice the banana.

   Blending Process:
   - In a blender, combine the mixed berries, sliced banana, vanilla-flavored Greek yogurt, almond milk, vanilla extract, and honey or agave syrup (if using).

   Optional Add-ins:
   - For added nutrients, you can include a handful of spinach. If desired, add chia seeds for extra texture and nutrition.

   Blend until Smooth:
   - Blend all the ingredients until you achieve a smooth and delightful Vanilla Berry Delight Smoothie.

   Adjust Sweetness:
   - Taste the smoothie and adjust the sweetness by adding more honey or agave syrup if needed.

   Optional Ice:
   - Add ice cubes to the blender and blend again for a chilled and refreshing texture.

   Serve:
   - Pour the Vanilla Berry Delight Smoothie into a glass.

Optional Garnish:
- Garnish with a few whole berries or a sprinkle of chia seeds for an extra visual appeal.

Enjoy:
- Sip and enjoy the luscious blend of vanilla and mixed berries in the Vanilla Berry Delight Smoothie!

Feel free to customize the recipe to suit your taste preferences. This smoothie combines the sweetness of mixed berries with the creamy and aromatic touch of vanilla. Whether it's for breakfast, a snack, or a sweet treat, the Vanilla Berry Delight Smoothie is sure to satisfy your cravings. Cheers to a delightful and berry-filled blend!

Green Tea Mango Fusion

Ingredients:

- 1 green tea bag
- 1 cup hot water
- 1 cup frozen mango chunks
- 1/2 banana, peeled and sliced
- 1/2 cup Greek yogurt (or any yogurt of your choice)
- 1 tablespoon honey or agave syrup (optional, for added sweetness)
- Ice cubes

Optional Add-ins:

- Fresh mint leaves for added freshness
- Chia seeds for extra texture and nutrition
- A squeeze of lime juice for a citrusy kick

Instructions:

Prepare Green Tea:
- Steep the green tea bag in hot water according to the package instructions. Allow it to cool.

Blending Process:
- In a blender, combine the frozen mango chunks, sliced banana, Greek yogurt, cooled green tea, and honey or agave syrup (if using).

Optional Add-ins:
- For added freshness, include fresh mint leaves. If desired, add chia seeds for extra texture and nutrition or a squeeze of lime juice for a citrusy kick.

Blend until Smooth:
- Blend all the ingredients until you achieve a smooth and invigorating Green Tea Mango Fusion.

Adjust Sweetness:
- Taste the fusion and adjust the sweetness by adding more honey or agave syrup if needed.

Optional Ice:
- Add ice cubes to the blender and blend again for a chilled and refreshing texture.

Serve:
- Pour the Green Tea Mango Fusion into a glass.

Optional Garnish:

- Garnish with a slice of mango or a sprig of fresh mint for an extra touch.

Enjoy:
- Sip and savor the delightful combination of green tea and mango in the Green Tea Mango Fusion!

Feel free to customize the recipe based on your preferences. This fusion combines the antioxidant benefits of green tea with the tropical sweetness of mango for a refreshing and healthful beverage. Whether it's for a morning pick-me-up or an afternoon refresher, the Green Tea Mango Fusion is a delicious and energizing choice. Cheers to a flavorful fusion!

Peanut Butter Banana Power

Ingredients:

- 1 banana, peeled and sliced
- 2 tablespoons peanut butter (preferably natural)
- 1 cup almond milk (or any milk of your choice)
- 1/2 cup Greek yogurt (or any yogurt of your choice)
- 1 tablespoon honey or maple syrup (optional, for added sweetness)
- 1/2 teaspoon cinnamon
- Ice cubes

Optional Add-ins:

- A scoop of protein powder for extra power
- Chia seeds for added texture and nutrition
- Oats for additional fiber and sustained energy

Instructions:

Prepare Ingredients:
- Peel and slice the banana.

Blending Process:
- In a blender, combine the sliced banana, peanut butter, almond milk, Greek yogurt, honey or maple syrup (if using), and cinnamon.

Optional Add-ins:
- For an extra power boost, add a scoop of protein powder. If desired, include chia seeds for added texture and nutrition, or oats for additional fiber and sustained energy.

Blend until Smooth:
- Blend all the ingredients until you achieve a smooth and powerful Peanut Butter Banana Power Smoothie.

Adjust Sweetness:
- Taste the smoothie and adjust the sweetness by adding more honey or maple syrup if needed.

Optional Ice:
- Add ice cubes to the blender and blend again for a chilled and refreshing texture.

Serve:
- Pour the Peanut Butter Banana Power Smoothie into a glass.

Optional Garnish:
- Garnish with a sprinkle of cinnamon or a drizzle of peanut butter for an extra flavorful touch.

Enjoy:
- Sip and relish the powerful combination of peanut butter and banana in the Peanut Butter Banana Power Smoothie!

Feel free to customize the recipe based on your preferences and dietary needs. This smoothie is not only delicious but also packed with protein, healthy fats, and natural sweetness from the banana. Whether it's for a pre-workout boost or a satisfying breakfast, the Peanut Butter Banana Power Smoothie is sure to provide a tasty and energizing experience. Cheers to a powerful blend!

Orange Carrot Turmeric Elixir

Ingredients:

- 2 large carrots, peeled and chopped
- 1 orange, peeled and segmented
- 1-inch piece of fresh turmeric, peeled and chopped (or 1 teaspoon ground turmeric)
- 1/2 inch piece of fresh ginger, peeled and chopped
- 1 tablespoon honey or agave syrup (optional, for added sweetness)
- 1 cup water
- Ice cubes

Optional Add-ins:

- A pinch of black pepper (enhances turmeric absorption)
- Fresh mint leaves for added freshness
- Chia seeds for extra texture and nutrition

Instructions:

    Prepare Ingredients:
- Peel and chop the carrots.
- Peel and segment the orange.
- Peel and chop the fresh turmeric and ginger.

    Blending Process:
- In a blender, combine the chopped carrots, orange segments, fresh turmeric, fresh ginger, honey or agave syrup (if using), and water.

    Optional Add-ins:
- For enhanced turmeric absorption, add a pinch of black pepper. If desired, include fresh mint leaves for added freshness or chia seeds for extra texture and nutrition.

    Blend until Smooth:
- Blend all the ingredients until you achieve a smooth and vibrant Orange Carrot Turmeric Elixir.

    Adjust Sweetness:
- Taste the elixir and adjust the sweetness by adding more honey or agave syrup if needed.

    Optional Strain:
- If you prefer a smoother texture, you can strain the elixir using a fine mesh sieve or cheesecloth.

Optional Ice:
- Add ice cubes to the blender and blend again for a chilled and refreshing elixir.

Serve:
- Pour the Orange Carrot Turmeric Elixir into a glass.

Optional Garnish:
- Garnish with a slice of orange or a sprig of fresh mint for an extra touch.

Enjoy:
- Sip and enjoy the nourishing and immune-boosting qualities of the Orange Carrot Turmeric Elixir!

Feel free to customize the recipe to your liking. This elixir combines the sweetness of carrots and oranges with the anti-inflammatory properties of turmeric and the zing of fresh ginger. Whether it's a morning wellness routine or an afternoon pick-me-up, this elixir is a vibrant and nutritious choice. Cheers to a refreshing and healthful blend!

Chocolate Banana Nut Smoothie

Ingredients:

- 1 banana, peeled and sliced
- 1 cup almond milk (or any milk of your choice)
- 1 tablespoon almond butter
- 1 tablespoon cocoa powder
- 1 tablespoon chopped nuts (walnuts, almonds, or hazelnuts)
- 1 tablespoon honey or maple syrup (optional, for added sweetness)
- Ice cubes

Optional Add-ins:

- A scoop of chocolate protein powder for extra protein
- Chia seeds for added texture and nutrition
- Greek yogurt for added creaminess

Instructions:

Prepare Ingredients:
- Peel and slice the banana.
- Chop the nuts.

Blending Process:
- In a blender, combine the sliced banana, almond milk, almond butter, cocoa powder, chopped nuts, and honey or maple syrup (if using).

Optional Add-ins:
- For extra protein, add a scoop of chocolate protein powder. If desired, include chia seeds for added texture and nutrition or Greek yogurt for added creaminess.

Blend until Smooth:
- Blend all the ingredients until you achieve a smooth and indulgent Chocolate Banana Nut Smoothie.

Adjust Sweetness:
- Taste the smoothie and adjust the sweetness by adding more honey or maple syrup if needed.

Optional Ice:
- Add ice cubes to the blender and blend again for a chilled and refreshing texture.

Serve:
- Pour the Chocolate Banana Nut Smoothie into a glass.

Optional Garnish:
- Garnish with a sprinkle of chopped nuts or a drizzle of chocolate syrup for an extra treat.

Enjoy:
- Sip and relish the delightful combination of chocolate, banana, and nuts in the Chocolate Banana Nut Smoothie!

Feel free to customize the recipe based on your preferences. This smoothie offers a rich and nutty flavor with the sweetness of banana and the indulgence of chocolate. Whether it's for breakfast, a snack, or a post-workout treat, the Chocolate Banana Nut Smoothie is sure to satisfy your cravings. Cheers to a delicious and nutty blend!

Mango Coconut Chia Delight

Ingredients:

- 1 cup frozen or fresh mango chunks
- 1/2 cup coconut milk
- 1/2 cup Greek yogurt (or coconut yogurt for a dairy-free option)
- 2 tablespoons chia seeds
- 1 tablespoon honey or agave syrup (optional, for added sweetness)
- 1/2 teaspoon vanilla extract
- Ice cubes

Optional Add-ins:

- Shredded coconut for added texture
- A squeeze of lime juice for a citrusy kick
- Fresh mint leaves for freshness

Instructions:

Prepare Ingredients:
- If using fresh mango, cut it into chunks.

Blending Process:
- In a blender, combine the mango chunks, coconut milk, Greek yogurt, chia seeds, honey or agave syrup (if using), and vanilla extract.

Optional Add-ins:
- For added texture, you can include shredded coconut. If desired, add a squeeze of lime juice for a citrusy kick or fresh mint leaves for freshness.

Blend until Smooth:
- Blend all the ingredients until you achieve a smooth and tropical Mango Coconut Chia Delight.

Adjust Sweetness:
- Taste the smoothie and adjust the sweetness by adding more honey or agave syrup if needed.

Optional Ice:
- Add ice cubes to the blender and blend again for a chilled and refreshing texture.

Serve:
- Pour the Mango Coconut Chia Delight into a glass.

Optional Garnish:
- Garnish with a sprinkle of shredded coconut or a slice of mango for an extra tropical touch.

Enjoy:

- Sip and savor the tropical and chia goodness of the Mango Coconut Chia Delight!

Feel free to customize the recipe based on your preferences. This smoothie combines the tropical flavors of mango and coconut with the nutritional benefits of chia seeds. Whether it's for breakfast, a snack, or a light dessert, the Mango Coconut Chia Delight is a refreshing and nutritious choice. Cheers to a delightful and tropical blend!

Pineapple Spinach Sunshine

Ingredients:

- 1 cup fresh spinach leaves, washed
- 1 cup frozen or fresh pineapple chunks
- 1 banana, peeled and sliced
- 1/2 cup coconut water (or water)
- 1/2 cup Greek yogurt (or any yogurt of your choice)
- 1 tablespoon chia seeds
- 1 tablespoon honey or agave syrup (optional, for added sweetness)
- Ice cubes

Optional Add-ins:

- A splash of lime juice for a citrusy kick
- Fresh mint leaves for added freshness
- Flaxseeds for added Omega-3s

Instructions:

Prepare Ingredients:
- Wash the spinach leaves.
- If using fresh pineapple, cut it into chunks.
- Peel and slice the banana.

Blending Process:
- In a blender, combine the fresh spinach leaves, pineapple chunks, sliced banana, coconut water, Greek yogurt, chia seeds, and honey or agave syrup (if using).

Optional Add-ins:
- For a citrusy kick, add a splash of lime juice. If desired, include fresh mint leaves for added freshness or flaxseeds for added Omega-3s.

Blend until Smooth:
- Blend all the ingredients until you achieve a smooth and vibrant Pineapple Spinach Sunshine Smoothie.

Adjust Sweetness:
- Taste the smoothie and adjust the sweetness by adding more honey or agave syrup if needed.

Optional Ice:
- Add ice cubes to the blender and blend again for a chilled and refreshing texture.

Serve:
- Pour the Pineapple Spinach Sunshine Smoothie into a glass.

Optional Garnish:

- Garnish with a slice of pineapple or a sprig of fresh mint for an extra tropical touch.

Enjoy:
- Sip and enjoy the sunny and nutrient-packed goodness of the Pineapple Spinach Sunshine Smoothie!

Feel free to customize the recipe based on your taste preferences. This smoothie combines the tropical sweetness of pineapple with the nutritional powerhouse of spinach, creating a refreshing and healthy drink. Whether it's for breakfast, a snack, or a post-workout refuel, the Pineapple Spinach Sunshine Smoothie is a delightful choice. Cheers to a sunshine-filled blend!

Banana Berry Protein Boost

Ingredients:

- 1 banana, peeled and sliced
- 1/2 cup mixed berries (strawberries, blueberries, raspberries)
- 1/2 cup Greek yogurt (or any yogurt of your choice)
- 1/2 cup almond milk (or any milk of your choice)
- 1 scoop vanilla protein powder
- 1 tablespoon almond butter
- 1 tablespoon honey or agave syrup (optional, for added sweetness)
- Ice cubes

Optional Add-ins:

- A handful of spinach for added nutrients
- Chia seeds for extra texture and nutrition
- Oats for additional fiber and sustained energy

Instructions:

Prepare Ingredients:
- Peel and slice the banana.
- If using fresh berries, wash them thoroughly.

Blending Process:
- In a blender, combine the sliced banana, mixed berries, Greek yogurt, almond milk, vanilla protein powder, almond butter, and honey or agave syrup (if using).

Optional Add-ins:
- For added nutrients, you can include a handful of spinach. If desired, add chia seeds for extra texture and nutrition or oats for additional fiber and sustained energy.

Blend until Smooth:
- Blend all the ingredients until you achieve a smooth and protein-packed Banana Berry Protein Boost.

Adjust Sweetness:
- Taste the smoothie and adjust the sweetness by adding more honey or agave syrup if needed.

Optional Ice:
- Add ice cubes to the blender and blend again for a chilled and refreshing texture.

Serve:
- Pour the Banana Berry Protein Boost Smoothie into a glass.

Optional Garnish:

- Garnish with a few whole berries or a sprinkle of chia seeds for an extra touch.

Enjoy:
- Sip and relish the protein-rich goodness of the Banana Berry Protein Boost Smoothie!

Feel free to customize the recipe based on your preferences and dietary needs. This smoothie is a great option for a post-workout recovery or a nutritious breakfast. The combination of banana, berries, and protein provides a delicious and satisfying blend. Cheers to a tasty and protein-packed boost!

Cherry Almond Smoothie

Ingredients:

- 1 cup frozen or fresh cherries, pitted
- 1 banana, peeled and sliced
- 1/2 cup almond milk (or any milk of your choice)
- 1/2 cup Greek yogurt (or any yogurt of your choice)
- 2 tablespoons almond butter
- 1 tablespoon honey or maple syrup (optional, for added sweetness)
- Ice cubes

Optional Add-ins:

- A handful of spinach for added nutrients
- Chia seeds for extra texture and nutrition
- A splash of vanilla extract for additional flavor

Instructions:

Prepare Ingredients:
- If using fresh cherries, pit them.
- Peel and slice the banana.

Blending Process:
- In a blender, combine the cherries, sliced banana, almond milk, Greek yogurt, almond butter, and honey or maple syrup (if using).

Optional Add-ins:
- For added nutrients, you can include a handful of spinach. If desired, add chia seeds for extra texture and nutrition or a splash of vanilla extract for additional flavor.

Blend until Smooth:
- Blend all the ingredients until you achieve a smooth and luscious Cherry Almond Smoothie.

Adjust Sweetness:
- Taste the smoothie and adjust the sweetness by adding more honey or maple syrup if needed.

Optional Ice:
- Add ice cubes to the blender and blend again for a chilled and refreshing texture.

Serve:
- Pour the Cherry Almond Smoothie into a glass.

Optional Garnish:

- Garnish with a few whole cherries or a sprinkle of sliced almonds for an extra touch.

Enjoy:
- Sip and savor the delightful combination of cherries and almonds in the Cherry Almond Smoothie!

Feel free to customize the recipe based on your preferences. This smoothie offers a sweet and nutty flavor with the richness of almond butter and the natural sweetness of cherries. Whether it's for breakfast, a snack, or a post-workout refuel, the Cherry Almond Smoothie is a tasty and nutritious choice. Cheers to a delicious and cherry-filled blend!

Mocha Banana Coffee

Ingredients:

- 1 banana, peeled and sliced
- 1/2 cup strong brewed coffee, cooled
- 1/2 cup almond milk (or any milk of your choice)
- 1 tablespoon cocoa powder
- 1 tablespoon almond butter
- 1 tablespoon honey or maple syrup (optional, for added sweetness)
- Ice cubes

Optional Add-ins:

- A scoop of chocolate protein powder for extra protein
- Chia seeds for added texture and nutrition
- A dash of cinnamon for enhanced flavor

Instructions:

Prepare Ingredients:
- Peel and slice the banana.

Blending Process:
- In a blender, combine the sliced banana, cooled brewed coffee, almond milk, cocoa powder, almond butter, and honey or maple syrup (if using).

Optional Add-ins:
- For extra protein, add a scoop of chocolate protein powder. If desired, include chia seeds for added texture and nutrition or a dash of cinnamon for enhanced flavor.

Blend until Smooth:
- Blend all the ingredients until you achieve a smooth and energizing Mocha Banana Coffee Smoothie.

Adjust Sweetness:
- Taste the smoothie and adjust the sweetness by adding more honey or maple syrup if needed.

Optional Ice:
- Add ice cubes to the blender and blend again for a chilled and refreshing texture.

Serve:
- Pour the Mocha Banana Coffee Smoothie into a glass.

Optional Garnish:

- Garnish with a sprinkle of cocoa powder or a few coffee beans for an extra coffee-inspired touch.

Enjoy:
- Sip and enjoy the delightful combination of mocha, banana, and coffee in the Mocha Banana Coffee Smoothie!

Feel free to customize the recipe based on your taste preferences. This smoothie combines the rich flavors of coffee and cocoa with the sweetness of banana, creating a delicious and caffeinated treat. Whether it's for a morning pick-me-up or an afternoon indulgence, the Mocha Banana Coffee Smoothie is sure to satisfy your coffee cravings. Cheers to a mocha-infused blend!

Raspberry Mango Coconut Dream

Ingredients:

- 1 cup frozen or fresh raspberries
- 1 cup frozen or fresh mango chunks
- 1/2 cup coconut milk
- 1/2 cup Greek yogurt (or any yogurt of your choice)
- 1 tablespoon shredded coconut
- 1 tablespoon honey or agave syrup (optional, for added sweetness)
- Ice cubes

Optional Add-ins:

- A splash of lime juice for a citrusy kick
- Chia seeds for extra texture and nutrition
- Fresh mint leaves for added freshness

Instructions:

Prepare Ingredients:
- If using fresh raspberries and mango, wash them thoroughly and cut into chunks.

Blending Process:
- In a blender, combine the raspberries, mango chunks, coconut milk, Greek yogurt, shredded coconut, and honey or agave syrup (if using).

Optional Add-ins:
- For a citrusy kick, add a splash of lime juice. If desired, include chia seeds for extra texture and nutrition or fresh mint leaves for added freshness.

Blend until Smooth:
- Blend all the ingredients until you achieve a smooth and tropical Raspberry Mango Coconut Dream Smoothie.

Adjust Sweetness:
- Taste the smoothie and adjust the sweetness by adding more honey or agave syrup if needed.

Optional Ice:
- Add ice cubes to the blender and blend again for a chilled and refreshing texture.

Serve:
- Pour the Raspberry Mango Coconut Dream Smoothie into a glass.

Optional Garnish:

- Garnish with a sprinkle of shredded coconut or a slice of mango for an extra tropical touch.

Enjoy:
- Sip and savor the dreamy combination of raspberry, mango, and coconut in the Raspberry Mango Coconut Dream Smoothie!

Feel free to customize the recipe based on your preferences. This smoothie offers a tropical blend with the sweetness of mango, the tartness of raspberries, and the creaminess of coconut. Whether it's for breakfast, a snack, or a refreshing treat, the Raspberry Mango Coconut Dream Smoothie is a delightful choice. Cheers to a dreamy and tropical fusion!

Green Avocado Pineapple Powerhouse

Ingredients:

- 1/2 ripe avocado, peeled and pitted
- 1 cup fresh or frozen pineapple chunks
- Handful of fresh spinach leaves
- 1/2 banana, peeled and sliced
- 1/2 cup coconut water (or water)
- 1/2 cup Greek yogurt (or any yogurt of your choice)
- 1 tablespoon chia seeds
- 1 tablespoon honey or agave syrup (optional, for added sweetness)
- Ice cubes

Optional Add-ins:

- A splash of lime juice for a citrusy kick
- Flaxseeds for additional fiber and Omega-3s
- Fresh mint leaves for added freshness

Instructions:

Prepare Ingredients:
- Peel and pit the avocado.
- If using fresh pineapple, cut it into chunks.
- Peel and slice the banana.

Blending Process:
- In a blender, combine the ripe avocado, pineapple chunks, fresh spinach leaves, sliced banana, coconut water, Greek yogurt, chia seeds, and honey or agave syrup (if using).

Optional Add-ins:
- For a citrusy kick, add a splash of lime juice. If desired, include flaxseeds for additional fiber and Omega-3s or fresh mint leaves for added freshness.

Blend until Smooth:
- Blend all the ingredients until you achieve a smooth and vibrant Green Avocado Pineapple Powerhouse Smoothie.

Adjust Sweetness:
- Taste the smoothie and adjust the sweetness by adding more honey or agave syrup if needed.

Optional Ice:
- Add ice cubes to the blender and blend again for a chilled and refreshing texture.

Serve:

- Pour the Green Avocado Pineapple Powerhouse Smoothie into a glass.

Optional Garnish:
- Garnish with a slice of pineapple or a sprig of fresh mint for an extra touch.

Enjoy:
- Sip and relish the nutrient-packed goodness of the Green Avocado Pineapple Powerhouse Smoothie!

Feel free to customize the recipe based on your preferences. This smoothie combines the creamy texture of avocado with the tropical sweetness of pineapple, creating a powerhouse of nutrients. Whether it's for breakfast, a post-workout refuel, or a refreshing snack, the Green Avocado Pineapple Powerhouse Smoothie is a nourishing and delicious choice. Cheers to a green and powerful blend!

Blueberry Walnut Bliss

Ingredients:

- 1 cup frozen or fresh blueberries
- 1/4 cup walnuts
- 1 banana, peeled and sliced
- 1/2 cup almond milk (or any milk of your choice)
- 1/2 cup Greek yogurt (or any yogurt of your choice)
- 1 tablespoon chia seeds
- 1 tablespoon honey or maple syrup (optional, for added sweetness)
- Ice cubes

Optional Add-ins:

- A sprinkle of cinnamon for enhanced flavor
- Flaxseeds for additional fiber and Omega-3s
- A handful of spinach for added nutrients

Instructions:

Prepare Ingredients:
- If using fresh blueberries, wash them thoroughly.
- Roughly chop the walnuts.
- Peel and slice the banana.

Blending Process:
- In a blender, combine the blueberries, walnuts, sliced banana, almond milk, Greek yogurt, chia seeds, and honey or maple syrup (if using).

Optional Add-ins:
- For enhanced flavor, add a sprinkle of cinnamon. If desired, include flaxseeds for additional fiber and Omega-3s or a handful of spinach for added nutrients.

Blend until Smooth:
- Blend all the ingredients until you achieve a smooth and blissful Blueberry Walnut Bliss Smoothie.

Adjust Sweetness:
- Taste the smoothie and adjust the sweetness by adding more honey or maple syrup if needed.

Optional Ice:
- Add ice cubes to the blender and blend again for a chilled and refreshing texture.

Serve:
- Pour the Blueberry Walnut Bliss Smoothie into a glass.

Optional Garnish:
- Garnish with a few whole blueberries or a sprinkle of chopped walnuts for an extra touch.

Enjoy:
- Sip and savor the delightful combination of blueberries and walnuts in the Blueberry Walnut Bliss Smoothie!

Feel free to customize the recipe based on your preferences. This smoothie offers a burst of antioxidants from blueberries and the heart-healthy goodness of walnuts. Whether it's for breakfast, a snack, or a post-workout treat, the Blueberry Walnut Bliss Smoothie is a delicious and nutritious choice. Cheers to a blissful and blueberry-filled blend!

Peach Raspberry Chia Refuel

Ingredients:

- 1 cup frozen or fresh peaches, sliced
- 1/2 cup frozen or fresh raspberries
- 1 tablespoon chia seeds
- 1/2 cup almond milk (or any milk of your choice)
- 1/2 cup Greek yogurt (or any yogurt of your choice)
- 1 tablespoon honey or agave syrup (optional, for added sweetness)
- Ice cubes

Optional Add-ins:

- A splash of orange juice for a citrusy kick
- Flaxseeds for additional fiber and Omega-3s
- A handful of spinach for added nutrients

Instructions:

Prepare Ingredients:
- If using fresh peaches, slice them.
- If using fresh raspberries, wash them thoroughly.

Blending Process:
- In a blender, combine the sliced peaches, raspberries, chia seeds, almond milk, Greek yogurt, and honey or agave syrup (if using).

Optional Add-ins:
- For a citrusy kick, add a splash of orange juice. If desired, include flaxseeds for additional fiber and Omega-3s or a handful of spinach for added nutrients.

Blend until Smooth:
- Blend all the ingredients until you achieve a smooth and refueling Peach Raspberry Chia Refuel Smoothie.

Adjust Sweetness:
- Taste the smoothie and adjust the sweetness by adding more honey or agave syrup if needed.

Optional Ice:
- Add ice cubes to the blender and blend again for a chilled and refreshing texture.

Serve:
- Pour the Peach Raspberry Chia Refuel Smoothie into a glass.

Optional Garnish:
- Garnish with a slice of peach or a few whole raspberries for an extra touch.

Enjoy:

- Sip and refuel with the nutritious and fruity goodness of the Peach Raspberry Chia Refuel Smoothie!

Feel free to customize the recipe based on your preferences. This smoothie combines the sweetness of peaches, the tartness of raspberries, and the nutritional benefits of chia seeds for a refueling and delicious blend. Whether it's for post-exercise recovery or a refreshing snack, the Peach Raspberry Chia Refuel Smoothie is a tasty and energizing choice. Cheers to a refueled and revitalized blend!

Pineapple Banana Turmeric

Ingredients:

- 1 cup frozen or fresh pineapple chunks
- 1 banana, peeled and sliced
- 1/2 teaspoon ground turmeric (or 1-inch piece of fresh turmeric, peeled and chopped)
- 1/2 cup coconut milk (or any milk of your choice)
- 1/2 cup Greek yogurt (or any yogurt of your choice)
- 1 tablespoon honey or agave syrup (optional, for added sweetness)
- Ice cubes

Optional Add-ins:

- A pinch of black pepper (enhances turmeric absorption)
- Chia seeds for extra texture and nutrition
- Fresh ginger for added warmth and flavor

Instructions:

Prepare Ingredients:
- If using fresh pineapple, cut it into chunks.
- Peel and slice the banana.
- If using fresh turmeric, peel and chop it.

Blending Process:
- In a blender, combine the pineapple chunks, sliced banana, ground turmeric (or fresh turmeric), coconut milk, Greek yogurt, and honey or agave syrup (if using).

Optional Add-ins:
- For enhanced turmeric absorption, add a pinch of black pepper. If desired, include chia seeds for extra texture and nutrition or fresh ginger for added warmth and flavor.

Blend until Smooth:
- Blend all the ingredients until you achieve a smooth and tropical Pineapple Banana Turmeric Smoothie.

Adjust Sweetness:
- Taste the smoothie and adjust the sweetness by adding more honey or agave syrup if needed.

Optional Ice:
- Add ice cubes to the blender and blend again for a chilled and refreshing texture.

Serve:
- Pour the Pineapple Banana Turmeric Smoothie into a glass.

Optional Garnish:

- Garnish with a slice of pineapple or a sprinkle of ground turmeric for an extra tropical touch.

Enjoy:
- Sip and relish the tropical and anti-inflammatory goodness of the Pineapple Banana Turmeric Smoothie!

Feel free to customize the recipe based on your preferences. This smoothie combines the tropical flavors of pineapple and banana with the anti-inflammatory properties of turmeric. Whether it's for breakfast, a snack, or a refreshing treat, the Pineapple Banana Turmeric Smoothie is a delicious and healthful choice. Cheers to a tropical and turmeric-infused blend!

Coconut Blue Spirulina Elixir

Ingredients:

- 1 cup coconut water
- 1/2 cup coconut milk
- 1 teaspoon blue spirulina powder
- 1 tablespoon honey or agave syrup (optional, for added sweetness)
- 1/2 teaspoon vanilla extract
- Ice cubes

Optional Add-ins:

- Chia seeds for extra texture and nutrition
- A splash of lime juice for a citrusy kick
- Fresh mint leaves for added freshness

Instructions:

Blending Process:
- In a blender, combine the coconut water, coconut milk, blue spirulina powder, honey or agave syrup (if using), and vanilla extract.

Optional Add-ins:
- For extra texture and nutrition, add chia seeds. If desired, include a splash of lime juice for a citrusy kick or fresh mint leaves for added freshness.

Blend until Smooth:
- Blend all the ingredients until you achieve a smooth and vibrant Coconut Blue Spirulina Elixir.

Adjust Sweetness:
- Taste the elixir and adjust the sweetness by adding more honey or agave syrup if needed.

Optional Ice:
- Add ice cubes to the blender and blend again for a chilled and refreshing texture.

Serve:
- Pour the Coconut Blue Spirulina Elixir into a glass.

Optional Garnish:
- Garnish with a sprinkle of blue spirulina powder or a slice of lime for an extra touch.

Enjoy:

- Sip and enjoy the hydrating and nutrient-packed goodness of the Coconut Blue Spirulina Elixir!

Feel free to customize the recipe based on your preferences. This elixir combines the tropical flavors of coconut with the vibrant and nutritious blue spirulina. Whether it's for a morning boost, an afternoon pick-me-up, or a post-workout refreshment, the Coconut Blue Spirulina Elixir is a refreshing and healthful choice. Cheers to a coconut-infused and blue spirulina elixir!

Orange Carrot Mango Glow

Ingredients:

- 1 cup fresh orange juice
- 1/2 cup carrot juice
- 1 cup frozen mango chunks
- 1/2 banana, peeled and sliced
- 1/2 cup Greek yogurt (or any yogurt of your choice)
- 1 tablespoon chia seeds
- 1 tablespoon honey or agave syrup (optional, for added sweetness)
- Ice cubes

Optional Add-ins:

- A pinch of turmeric for anti-inflammatory benefits
- Fresh ginger for added warmth and flavor
- Flaxseeds for additional fiber and Omega-3s

Instructions:

Prepare Ingredients:
- Squeeze fresh orange juice or use store-bought 100% orange juice.
- Extract carrot juice using a juicer or use store-bought carrot juice.
- Peel and slice the banana.

Blending Process:
- In a blender, combine the fresh orange juice, carrot juice, frozen mango chunks, sliced banana, Greek yogurt, chia seeds, and honey or agave syrup (if using).

Optional Add-ins:
- For anti-inflammatory benefits, add a pinch of turmeric. If desired, include fresh ginger for added warmth and flavor or flaxseeds for additional fiber and Omega-3s.

Blend until Smooth:
- Blend all the ingredients until you achieve a smooth and glowing Orange Carrot Mango Glow Smoothie.

Adjust Sweetness:
- Taste the smoothie and adjust the sweetness by adding more honey or agave syrup if needed.

Optional Ice:

- Add ice cubes to the blender and blend again for a chilled and refreshing texture.

Serve:
- Pour the Orange Carrot Mango Glow Smoothie into a glass.

Optional Garnish:
- Garnish with a slice of orange or a sprinkle of chia seeds for an extra touch.

Enjoy:
- Sip and revel in the vibrant and nutritious goodness of the Orange Carrot Mango Glow Smoothie!

Feel free to customize the recipe based on your preferences. This smoothie combines the refreshing flavors of orange, the earthy sweetness of carrot, and the tropical goodness of mango for a glowing and nutrient-packed blend. Whether it's for breakfast, a midday pick-me-up, or a post-workout refuel, the Orange Carrot Mango Glow Smoothie is a delicious and rejuvenating choice. Cheers to a glowing and nutritious smoothie!

Chocolate Cherry Protein

Ingredients:

- 1 cup frozen or fresh cherries, pitted
- 1 cup almond milk (or any milk of your choice)
- 1 scoop chocolate protein powder
- 1 tablespoon almond butter
- 1 tablespoon cocoa powder
- 1 tablespoon honey or maple syrup (optional, for added sweetness)
- Ice cubes

Optional Add-ins:

- A handful of spinach for added nutrients
- Chia seeds for extra texture and nutrition
- Greek yogurt for creaminess

Instructions:

    Prepare Ingredients:
- If using fresh cherries, pit them.

    Blending Process:
- In a blender, combine the pitted cherries, almond milk, chocolate protein powder, almond butter, cocoa powder, and honey or maple syrup (if using).

    Optional Add-ins:
- For added nutrients, you can include a handful of spinach. If desired, add chia seeds for extra texture and nutrition or Greek yogurt for creaminess.

    Blend until Smooth:
- Blend all the ingredients until you achieve a smooth and chocolatey Cherry Protein Smoothie.

    Adjust Sweetness:
- Taste the smoothie and adjust the sweetness by adding more honey or maple syrup if needed.

    Optional Ice:
- Add ice cubes to the blender and blend again for a chilled and refreshing texture.

    Serve:
- Pour the Chocolate Cherry Protein Smoothie into a glass.

    Optional Garnish:
- Garnish with a few whole cherries or a sprinkle of cocoa powder for an extra touch.

    Enjoy:

- Sip and relish the delicious and protein-packed goodness of the Chocolate Cherry Protein Smoothie!

Feel free to customize the recipe based on your preferences. This smoothie combines the rich flavors of chocolate and cherries with the protein boost from protein powder and almond butter. Whether it's for a post-workout recovery or a satisfying breakfast, the Chocolate Cherry Protein Smoothie is a tasty and nutritious choice. Cheers to a chocolatey and protein-rich blend!

Raspberry Spinach Almond Bliss

Ingredients:

- 1 cup fresh or frozen raspberries
- Handful of fresh spinach leaves
- 1/4 cup almonds, preferably soaked
- 1 banana, peeled and sliced
- 1 cup almond milk (or any milk of your choice)
- 1 tablespoon chia seeds
- 1 tablespoon honey or agave syrup (optional, for added sweetness)
- Ice cubes

Optional Add-ins:

- A splash of vanilla extract for enhanced flavor
- Flaxseeds for additional fiber and Omega-3s
- Greek yogurt for creaminess

Instructions:

Prepare Ingredients:
- If using fresh raspberries, wash them thoroughly.
- Soak almonds in water for a few hours or overnight, then drain.

Blending Process:
- In a blender, combine the raspberries, fresh spinach leaves, soaked almonds, sliced banana, almond milk, chia seeds, and honey or agave syrup (if using).

Optional Add-ins:
- For enhanced flavor, add a splash of vanilla extract. If desired, include flaxseeds for additional fiber and Omega-3s or Greek yogurt for creaminess.

Blend until Smooth:
- Blend all the ingredients until you achieve a smooth and blissful Raspberry Spinach Almond Bliss Smoothie.

Adjust Sweetness:
- Taste the smoothie and adjust the sweetness by adding more honey or agave syrup if needed.

Optional Ice:
- Add ice cubes to the blender and blend again for a chilled and refreshing texture.

Serve:
- Pour the Raspberry Spinach Almond Bliss Smoothie into a glass.

Optional Garnish:
- Garnish with a few whole raspberries or a sprinkle of sliced almonds for an extra touch.

Enjoy:
- Sip and delight in the nutty, fruity, and nutritious goodness of the Raspberry Spinach Almond Bliss Smoothie!

Feel free to customize the recipe based on your preferences. This smoothie combines the sweetness of raspberries, the nutritional boost from spinach, and the nutty flavor of almonds. Whether it's for breakfast, a snack, or a post-workout refuel, the Raspberry Spinach Almond Bliss Smoothie is a delicious and nourishing choice. Cheers to a blissful and almond-infused blend!

www.ingramcontent.com/pod-product-compliance
Lightning Source LLC
LaVergne TN
LVHW081553060526
838201LV00054B/1884